Up & Running Series from SYBEX

MW00716416

Look for Up & Running books on a variety of popular software topics. Current titles include:

Up & Running with **AutoSketch 3**

Up & Running with **Carbon Copy Plus**

Up & Running with **DOS 3.3**

Up & Running with **DR DOS 5.0**

Up & Running with **Flight Simulator**

Up & Running with **Harvard Graphics**

Up & Running with **Lotus 1-2-3 Release 2.2**

Up & Running with **Lotus 1-2-3 Release 3.1**

Up & Running with **Norton Utilities**

Up & Running with **Norton Utilities 5**

Up & Running with **PageMaker 4 on the PC**

Up & Running with **PageMaker on the Macintosh**

Up & Running with **PC Tools Deluxe 6**

Up & Running with **PC-Write**

Up & Running with **PROCOMM PLUS**

Up & Running with **Q & A**

Up & Running with **Quicken 4**

Up & Running with **ToolBook for Windows**

Up & Running with **Turbo Pascal 5.5**

Up & Running with **Windows 3.0**

Up & Running with **Windows 286/386**

Up & Running with **WordPerfect 5.1**

Up & Running with **WordPerfect Library/Office PC**

Up & Running with **XTreeGold 2**

Up & Running with **Your Hard Disk**

Computer users are not all alike.
Neither are SYBEX books.

We know our customers have a variety of needs. They've told us so. And because we've listened, we've developed several distinct types of books to meet the needs of each of our customers. What are you looking for in computer help?

If you're looking for the basics, try the **ABC's** series. You'll find short, unintimidating tutorials and helpful illustrations. For a more visual approach, select **Teach Yourself**, featuring screen-by-screen illustrations of how to use your latest software purchase.

Mastering and **Understanding** titles offer you a step-by-step introduction, plus an in-depth examination of intermediate-level features, to use as you progress.

Our **Up & Running** series is designed for computer-literate consumers who want a no-nonsense overview of new programs. Just 20 basic lessons, and you're on your way.

We also publish two types of reference books. Our **Instant References** provide quick access to each of a program's commands and functions. SYBEX **Encyclopedias** provide a *comprehensive reference* and explanation of all of the commands, features and functions of the subject software.

Sometimes a subject requires a special treatment that our standard series doesn't provide. So you'll find we have titles like **Advanced Techniques, Handbooks, Tips & Tricks**, and others that are specifically tailored to satisfy a unique need.

We carefully select our authors for their in-depth understanding of the software they're writing about, as well as their ability to write clearly and communicate effectively. Each manuscript is thoroughly reviewed by our technical staff to ensure its complete accuracy. Our production department makes sure it's easy to use. All of this adds up to the highest quality books available, consistently appearing on best-seller charts worldwide.

You'll find SYBEX publishes a variety of books on every popular software package. Looking for computer help? Help Yourself to SYBEX.

For a complete catalog of our publications:

SYBEX Inc.

2021 Challenger Drive, Alameda, CA 94501

Tel: (415) 523-8233/(800) 227-2346 Telex: 336311

SYBEX Fax: (415) 523-2373

Up & Running with Quattro® Pro 3

Second Edition

Peter G. Aitken

SYBEX®

San Francisco • Paris • Düsseldorf • Soest

Acquisitions Editor: David Clark
Series Editor: Joanne Cuthbertson
Copy Editor: Brendan Fletcher
Technical Editor: Glen Y. Saika
Word Processors: Ann Dunn, Paul Erickson, Lisa Mitchell
Book Designer: Elke Hermanowski
Icon Designer: Helen Bruno
Screen Graphics: Cuong Le
Desktop Production Artist: Charlotte Carter
Proofreader: Carolina Montilla
Indexer: Ted Laux
Cover Designer: Archer Design

SYBEX is a registered trademark of SYBEX, Inc.

TRADEMARKS: SYBEX has attempted throughout this book to distinguish
proprietary trademarks from descriptive terms by following the capitalization
style used by the manufacturer.

SYBEX is not affiliated with any manufacturer.

Every effort has been made to supply complete and accurate information.
However, SYBEX assumes no responsibility for its use, nor for any infringe-
ment of the intellectual property rights of third parties which would result
from such use.

First edition copyright © 1991 SYBEX Inc.

Copyright ©1991 SYBEX Inc., 2021 Challenger Drive, Alameda, CA 94501.
World rights reserved. No part of this publication may be stored in a retrieval
system, transmitted, or reproduced in any way, including but not limited to
photocopy, photograph, magnetic or other record, without the prior agreement
and written permission of the publisher.

Library of Congress Card Number: 91-65407
ISBN: 0-89588-857-2

Manufactured in the United States of America
10 9 8 7 6 5 4 3 2 1

SYBEX
Up & Running Books

The Up & Running series of books from SYBEX has been developed for committed, eager PC users who would like to become familiar with a wide variety of programs and operations as quickly as possible. We assume that you are comfortable with your PC and that you know the basic functions of word processing, spreadsheets, and database management. With this background, Up & Running books will show you in 20 steps what particular products can do and how to use them.

Who this book is for

Up & Running books are designed to save you time and money. First, you can avoid purchase mistakes by previewing products before you buy them—exploring their features, strengths, and limitations. Second, once you decide to purchase a product, you can learn its basics quickly by following the 20 steps—even if you are a beginner.

What this book provides

The first step usually covers software installation in relation to hardware requirements. You'll learn whether the program can operate with your available hardware as well as various methods for starting the program. The second step often introduces the program's user interface. The remaining 18 steps demonstrate the program's basic functions, using examples and short descriptions.

Contents & structure

 A clock shows the amount of time you can expect to spend at your computer for each step. Naturally, you'll need much less time if you only read through the step rather than complete it at your computer.

Special symbols and notes

You can also focus on particular points by scanning the short notes in the margins and locating the sections you are most interested in.

In addition, three symbols highlight particular sections of text:

The Action symbol highlights important steps that you will carry out.

The Tip symbol indicates a practical hint or special technique.

The Warning symbol alerts you to a potential problem and suggestions for avoiding it.

We have structured the Up & Running books so that the busy user spends little time studying documentation and is not burdened with unnecessary text. An Up & Running book cannot, of course, replace a lengthier book that contains advanced applications. However, you will get the information you need to put the program to practical use and to learn its basic functions in the shortest possible time.

We welcome your comments

SYBEX is very interested in your reactions to the Up & Running series. Your opinions and suggestions will help all of our readers, including yourself. Please send your comments to: SYBEX Editorial Department, 2021 Challenger Drive, Alameda, CA 94501.

Preface

Release 3.0 is the latest version of Quattro Pro, Borland's powerful spreadsheet program. Packed with data-analysis and graphics features, Quattro Pro is a valuable time-saver for anyone who needs to work with numbers.

This book is intended to get you "up and running" with Quattro Pro as quickly as possible. Rather than covering every detail of the program, I present only the basic information you need to start doing productive work with Quattro Pro. All of the fundamentals are covered in 20 steps, starting with installation and working through data entry, formulas, graphics, and databases.

You can use this book no matter what your level of experience. If you're a total newcomer to spreadsheets, don't worry—I assume no previous knowledge on the part of the reader. If you have some experience with spreadsheets (either an earlier version of Quattro Pro or another program, such as Lotus 1-2-3), you may be able to skim some of the early steps and move quickly to the more advanced subjects.

If you're using version 2.0 of Quattro Pro, you can still use this book. The latest version, release 3.0, added some nice enhancements, but is otherwise almost identical to release 2.0. Where release 2.0 differs from release 3.0, it is indicated in the text with the notation *Version 2 users:*.

I think you'll enjoy using Quattro Pro. Once you have used it for awhile, you'll wonder how you ever got along without it!

Peter G. Aitken
Durham, North Carolina, April 1991

Table of Contents

Step 1

Installing Quattro Pro

This step describes the equipment needed to run Quattro Pro and shows you how to install Quattro Pro on your system. If you or somebody else has already installed Quattro Pro, you can skip ahead to Step 2.

Quattro Pro's Hardware and Software Requirements

To install and run Quattro Pro, you need at least the following:

- An IBM XT, AT, PS/2, or any 100%-compatible with 512K of memory (640K is recommended by Borland)

- DOS 2.0 or later

- One floppy-disk drive and a hard disk with at least 3Mb of free space

The following optional items of equipment will enhance Quattro Pro's operation:

Optional equipment

- To display graphs, you need a graphics card and monitor.

- To allow Quattro Pro to work with larger spreadsheets, you need expanded memory that conforms to the Lotus-Intel-Microsoft (LIM) 3.2 or 4.0 specification.

- To print spreadsheet data and graphs, you need a printer. Quattro Pro can work with a wide variety of printers.

- To perform spreadsheet tasks with a mouse, you need a Microsoft-compatible mouse. Many spreadsheet tasks are faster and easier with a mouse. Almost all mice, such as those from Logitech and Mouse Systems, can be used in Microsoft-compatible mode.

- To speed up certain mathematical calculations, you need a math coprocessor. If your system has a coprocessor, Quattro Pro automatically detects and uses it.

Installing Quattro Pro on Your System

Before installing Quattro Pro, you should make backup copies of the original disks to guard against accidental damage. Use the DOS DISKCOPY command to do this. When finished, keep the original disks in a safe place and use your backups for installation.

You cannot install Quattro Pro by simply copying files from the disks to your hard disk. You must use the installation program.

During installation, you will be asked to provide information on the manufacturer and model of your printer. Be sure you have this information available before starting. Then insert the Quattro Pro installation disk (number 1) in drive A. At the DOS prompt, type

```
a:install
```

and press Enter. If your system has a monochrome screen or you are installing on a laptop with an LCD display, type

```
a:install /b
```

to force the installation program to use black and white. The installation program will start and display its opening screen.

The installation process is quite straightforward, with clear explanations and instructions provided on-screen at every step. At most installation steps, pressing F2 brings up a list of choices. Move the highlight bar to the desired selection using the ↑ and ↓ keys, and press Enter to select it.

Select a printer mode

Toward the end of the installation process, you will be asked to select a printer mode. The exact modes available depend on the printer you selected earlier during installation. If you're not sure which mode to select, don't worry—you can always change printer modes later from within Quattro Pro.

Quattro Pro will also ask you to determine the number of fonts you would like to have generated. A *font* is a style and size of characters (letters, numbers, etc.) that Quattro Pro can use in printing spreadsheet data and graphs. Quattro Pro comes with a large number of fonts, but since each font takes up some disk space, you are given the option of generating all, some, or none of the fonts. Unless you are really short of disk space, I recommend that you install all of the fonts. You can, of course, both add and delete fonts later. Font generation takes some time. Depending on the number of fonts being generated and the speed of your computer, you may have time for a short coffee break!

Installing fonts

Viewing the README File

After installation is complete, you can consult a README file for information that, because of time limitations, couldn't be included in Quattro Pro's manuals. To view the README file, change to the Quattro Pro directory, then run the README program:

```
cd \qpro
readme
```

You can scroll through the information in the README file with the cursor keys and the PgUp and PgDn keys. When finished, press Esc to exit.

Quattro Pro Fundamentals

This step explains some fundamentals of operating Quattro Pro. You'll learn how to start Quattro Pro, use its menus, and access its help system. This step also describes the structure of a spreadsheet and the parts of the Quattro Pro screen.

Spreadsheet Structure

A *spreadsheet* can be described as a rectangular grid of cells. A *cell* is an independent location within the spreadsheet that can hold data of various kinds (more on this in the next step). Each cell is uniquely identified by its row and column position. Spreadsheet columns are identified by letters, and rows are identified by numbers. Thus the cell located at the intersection of column B and row 10 is referred to as cell B10.

A Quattro Pro spreadsheet has 8192 rows and 256 columns. The rows are numbered 1–8192 from top to bottom, and the columns are labeled with letters from left to right. The first 26 columns are labeled A–Z, the second 26 are labeled AA–AZ, the third 26 are BA–BZ, and so on up to the rightmost column, IV. A quick multiplication shows that a single Quattro Pro spreadsheet contains 2,097,152 cells.

A Quattro Pro spreadsheet contains over two million cells

Starting Quattro Pro

To start Quattro Pro, first change to the Quattro Pro directory, then enter the name of the program file. If you installed Quattro Pro in the directory \QPRO, type the following two commands, remembering to press Enter after each:

```
cd \qpro
q
```

Quattro Pro will load into memory, and the screen in Figure 2.1 will be displayed. If you have a color video system, the screen will be in color.

The Quattro Pro Screen

The components of the Quattro Pro screen are labeled in Figure 2.1. What follows is only a brief description of each. More detailed information will be provided later in the book as you need it.

- The *work area* contains the spreadsheet (which is blank in this figure). The column and row labels are displayed at the top and left of the work area. The *cell selector* is a moveable highlighted bar that indicates the current, or active, cell. Note that the work area can display only a small portion of the spreadsheet at one time, acting as a window onto the spreadsheet. In Figure 2.1, the cell selector is in cell A1.

- The *menu bar* displays the nine top-level entries on the pull-down menu tree.

- The *input line* displays information about the current cell and also displays data that is being entered or edited. Note

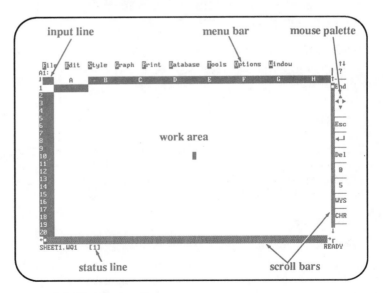

Figure 2.1: The Quattro Pro screen

that A1, the current cell's address, is displayed at the left of
the input line.

• The *scroll bars* indicate your vertical and horizontal position in the spreadsheet and are used to scroll around the
  spreadsheet with the mouse. Each scroll bar consists of a
  bar with an arrow at each end and a small box. You'll learn
  how to use the scroll bars in Step 3.

• The *status line* displays the name of the current spreadsheet
  file and, in brackets, the number of the current window
  (relevant when using multiple windows, which are covered
  in Step 14). In Figure 2.1 the file name SHEET1.WQ1 is
  displayed. This is a default file name assigned by Quattro
  Pro. At the right of the status line is the *mode indicator,*
  which displays the current spreadsheet mode. Other indica-
  tors, such as NumLock, are displayed here as well.

• The *mouse palette* is used to perform certain spreadsheet
  tasks using a mouse. The mouse palette is displayed only if
  you have a mouse installed.

Keyboard versus Mouse

While you don't need a mouse to use Quattro Pro, there's no
doubt that it makes some tasks quicker and easier. In this book
I will show you how to do things with both the mouse and the
keyboard.

If your system has a mouse installed, the Quattro Pro screen will
display the mouse palette and the *mouse pointer.* The mouse
pointer is a highlighted rectangle or arrow that appears on your
screen and moves when you move your mouse on the desktop.
If you're new to using a mouse, there are some terms you need
to know:

*The mouse
pointer*

• To *click* means to position the mouse pointer at a specific
  screen location and quickly press and release the mouse
  button. Unless directed otherwise, you click with the
  left button on the mouse.

Using the
mouse
palette

- To *drag* means to position the mouse pointer at a specific screen location, press the left mouse button, and move the mouse pointer to another screen location while keeping the button depressed. Then release the mouse button.

The items, or buttons, on the mouse palette let you enter certain commands or keystrokes with the mouse. The top two palette entries are fixed. Clicking the ? activates Quattro Pro's Help system, just as pressing F1 does. Clicking one of the arrowheads in the box labeled End is the same as pressing the End key followed by an arrow key. The remaining buttons are user-definable. Initially, the top three user-defined buttons are set up to duplicate the Esc key, the Enter key, and the Del key, respectively. The @button displays a list of @functions, from which you can select while writing a formula (@functions are Quattro Pro's built-in formulas, covered in Step 4). The buttons labeled WYS and CHR are used to switch between WYSIWYG display mode and character display mode (both modes will be explained in Step 7). The button labeled 5 is initially undefined. *Version 2 users:* The WYS and CHR buttons are not available; the equivalent buttons are labeled 6 and 7 and are initially undefined.

The uses of some of the mouse palette buttons may not be clear to you now, but you'll see how useful they can be as you work through the book (if you're using a mouse, that is).

Using the Menu System

QuattroPro
features
pull-down
menus

Quattro Pro's menu system utilizes a hierarchical tree structure. This means that each of the nine selections on the menu bar displays a pull-down menu containing additional selections. Each selection on a pull-down menu either performs an action or displays an additional pull-down menu. To execute most commands you must make between two and four sequential selections. Related commands are grouped together on the same "branch" of the menu tree.

To select a menu command, you must first display a pull-down menu from the menu bar. You can do this in two ways:

- If you are using a mouse, point to the desired item on the menu bar and click.

- If you are using the keyboard, press /. Then press the letter key corresponding to the first letter of the desired item, or use the ← and → keys to highlight the desired item and press Enter.

Go ahead and try it out—use the mouse or keyboard to select Edit from the menu bar. You will now see the pull-down menu shown in Figure 2.2. Note that while the menu system is active, the mode indicator displays MENU. In addition, the status line displays a brief description of the currently highlighted menu selection.

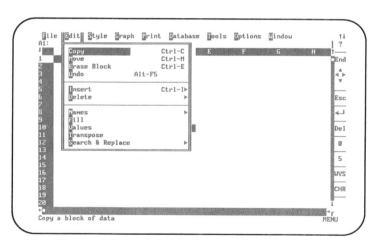

Figure 2.2: The Edit menu

An important key that you should know about is the Esc key, located at the upper left corner of most keyboards. You can think of Esc as the "back out" key. If you are entering data or executing a multistep menu command, pressing Esc backs you out of the process one step at a time, until you are back in READY mode. Esc can be a great help when you make a mistake during spreadsheet operations.

There are several features of pull-down menus you should know about:

- An arrowhead to the right of the command indicates that the command leads to another pull-down menu.

Use shortcut keys to save time

- A shortcut key is a way to select certain commands without using the menu system. Shortcut keys are provided for the most frequently used commands. For example, pressing Ctrl-C in READY mode has the same effect as selecting Copy from the Edit menu.

Menu commands

Throughout this book, menu commands are presented in the form /Edit|Insert|Rows. This means to select Edit from the menu bar, then select Insert from the first pull-down menu and Rows from the second pull-down menu.

The Help System

Quattro Pro has a sophisticated help system that makes it easy to obtain information about program operation while you are working. Help is context-sensitive, which means it displays information about the task you are performing when you activate Help. When you're not performing a specific task (i.e., when you are in READY mode), activating Help displays the main Help Topics screen, shown in Figure 2.3.

To use the Help system:

1. Press F1 or click the ? in the upper right corner of the screen.

2. If you are in READY mode, the Help Topics screen will appear (Figure 2.3).

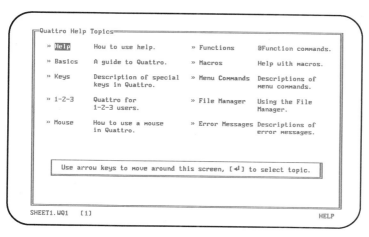

Figure 2.3: The Help Topics screen

3. If you are selecting from the menus or performing some task (such as editing a cell entry), a Help screen is displayed with information related to the task or highlighted menu command.

4. If desired, you can use the Help screen keywords to display Help on other topics. While using Help, press F1 if you need help on the Help system itself.

5. Press Esc to return to the spreadsheet.

All Quattro Pro Help screens contain a number of keywords that connect to related topics in the Help system. When you display a Help screen, the first keyword is highlighted (Help in Figure 2.3, for example). To move to a different Help topic, click the corresponding keyword, or use the ←, →, ↑, ↓, End, and Home keys to move the highlight to a specific keyword and press Enter. To exit Help, press Esc.

Help screen keywords

You are now ready to move on to Step 3. If you want to take a break, select /File|Exit to exit Quattro Pro and return to DOS.

Working with Data

This step shows you how to enter data into a Quattro Pro spreadsheet, how to edit data, and how to save your work in a disk file. If necessary, start Quattro Pro as explained in Step 2.

Moving around the Spreadsheet

The work area on your screen is like a window onto the entire spreadsheet; it can display only a small portion of the spreadsheet at one time. To view different regions of the spreadsheet you need to scroll the window. This is done by moving the cell selector. Quattro Pro always keeps the cell selector visible in the window. You can move the cell selector with the mouse or from the keyboard. At any time, the positions of the small boxes in the scroll bars indicate the vertical and horizontal position of the screen window relative to the active (i.e., data-containing) area of the spreadsheet.

To use the cursor keys to move around the spreadsheet, your keyboard's NumLock must be off.

- To move horizontally one cell, press the ← or → key or click the arrow at one end of the horizontal scroll bar.

- To move vertically one cell, press the ↓ or ↑ key or click the arrow at one end of the vertical scroll bar.

- To move horizontally one full screen, press Ctrl-→ or Ctrl-←, or click the horizontal scroll bar between the position box and one of the arrows.

- To move vertically one full screen, press PgUp or PgDn, or click the vertical scroll bar between the position box and one of the arrows.

- To move to cell A1, press Home.

- To move to a specific cell, press F5, type in the cell's address, and press Enter. Or, if the desired cell is visible in the window, simply click it.

*The
End key*

You can use the End key in conjunction with other keys for special moves. When you press and release End, the mode indicator displays END on the status line. To cancel, press End again.

- If the cell selector is on a blank cell, pressing End followed by an arrow key moves the cell selector to the first nonblank cell in the indicated direction or to the boundary of the spreadsheet.

- If the cell selector is on a nonblank cell, pressing End followed by an arrow key moves the cell selector to the cell immediately before the first blank cell in the indicated direction. If there is a blank or blanks after the nonblank starting point, then it will go to the next nonblank cell. Also, if there are no nonblanks, then the cursor will go to the spreadsheet boundary.

- From anywhere in the spreadsheet, pressing End followed by Home moves the cell selector to the last active cell. This cell is at the intersection of the last row and column that contain data.

You can also execute End-arrow commands by clicking one of the arrowheads in the End box on the mouse palette.

Quattro Pro will beep if you try to move the cell selector past the spreadsheet border.

Entering Data

*Labels
versus
values*

In this step, we will discuss two fundamental types of data that can be entered in a spreadsheet cell, numbers (also called values) and labels. Formulas, a third category of cell entry, are covered in Step 4.

- A *number* can contain any combination of digits 0–9. When you enter a number you can also include a decimal point, a trailing percent sign, a leading dollar sign, and a leading plus sign or minus sign.

- A *label* is text data, and can contain any combination of characters—letters, numbers, punctuation marks, etc. When a label is stored in a spreadsheet cell it is preceded by a *label prefix character* (explained below). The label prefix character is entered by the user or, in some cases, automatically by Quattro Pro.

To enter data in a spreadsheet cell:

1. Move the cell selector to the desired cell.

2. Type in the desired data. As you type, your entry is displayed in the input line, and the mode indicator displays either LABEL or VALUE depending on the data being entered.

3. If you make an error, press Backspace to erase it.

4. When finished, press Enter or move the cell selector to another cell.

5. To cancel your entry, press Esc before hitting Enter or an arrow key.

If your entry starts with a nonnumeric character, Quattro Pro assumes it's a label and automatically adds the default label prefix ('). If your entry starts with a numeric character, or when the first character is +, –, $, (, or @, Quattro Pro assumes it's a value and will not accept nonnumeric characters (e.g., if you enter **12 Oak St.**, Quattro will not accept **Oak Street**). To enter a label that starts with a numeric character, you must type the label prefix character yourself (e.g., type **'12 Oak St.**).

Label prefix characters

In addition to identifying a cell entry as a label, a label prefix character also controls how the label is displayed in the cell. You can type in any one of the four label prefix characters shown in Table 3.1, depending on your formatting needs.

Cell-entry alignment

Label Prefix Character	Effect
,	Left-aligns text in the cell.
"	Right-aligns text in the cell.
^	Centers text in the cell.
\	Repeats the following character(s) to fill the column width (used to create underlines, borders, etc.).

Table 3.1: The label prefix characters

Values are always displayed right-aligned. If a label is wider than the cell, one of two things happens:

- If the cell(s) to the right is empty, the full label is displayed.

- If the cell to the right is not empty, only as much of the label as will fit in the cell width is displayed (the entire label remains stored in the spreadsheet, however).

Label prefix characters do not display in the spreadsheet, but they are displayed in the input line when the cell selector is on a label cell.

Editing Data

When you edit, you are modifying data that is already entered into a spreadsheet cell. You can edit both label and value entries.

To edit data in a spreadsheet cell:

1. Move the cell selector to the desired cell.

2. Press the F2 (Edit) key. The mode indicator displays EDIT, and the cell's contents are displayed on the input line with the editing cursor at the end.

3. Use the ← and → keys to move the cursor one character at a time; use Ctrl-← and Ctrl-→ to move the cursor five

characters at a time. Use End and Home to move the cursor to the end or beginning of the data.

4. Press Backspace to delete the character to the left of the cursor. Press Del to delete the character under the cursor. Press Ctrl-\ to erase all characters to the right of the cursor. Press Escape to erase the entire entry.

5. Type in new characters as needed.

6. Press ↑, ↓, or Enter to accept the edited data.

7. Press Escape twice (before you press ↑, ↓, or Enter) to cancel editing and leave the original cell contents unchanged.

Working With Dates and Times

Quattro Pro displays dates and times in standard formats but stores them internally as serial numbers. The integer part of the serial number represents the date as the number of days since December 30, 1899. The fractional part of the serial number represents a fraction of the 24 hour day. This method greatly simplifies certain calculations, such as determining the number of days between two dates (simply subtract the two dates' serial numbers). Some examples appear in Table 3.2.

Quattro Pro stores dates as serial numbers

Date and/or time	Serial number
December 31, 1899	1
August 27, 1990	33112
12:00 Noon	0.5
9:00 PM (21:00)	0.75
4:48 AM on Feb 18, 1982	30000.2

Table 3.2: Sample dates and times with their corresponding serial numbers

You can enter a date or time into a cell in standard format, and Quattro Pro will automatically calculate the correct serial number.

To enter a date or time:

1. Move the cell selector to the desired cell.

2. Press Ctrl-D. The mode indicator will display DATE.

3. Enter a date or time in a standard format (see below), then press Enter or an arrow key.

4. Quattro Pro calculates the corresponding serial number and stores it in the cell. The cell displays the date or time in the format it was entered.

Date and time formats

Examples of the allowable date and time formats are shown below:

07-Mar-82

12-Jan (assumes current year)

Oct-85 (assumes first day of month)

17:30 (24 hour time)

11:45 PM (12 hour time)

The Undo Feature

Recovering from mistakes

What if you make a mistake while using Quattro Pro? The Undo feature lets you reverse your latest action, returning the spreadsheet to its previous state. Press Alt-F5 or select /Edit|Undo to execute Undo. Undo can reverse the following spreadsheet operations:

• Changing cell entries.

• Deleting a block name or a named graph.

• Retrieving a file.

• Erasing the current spreadsheets.

• Deleting, moving, or copying a block of cells.

Undo will not reverse changes to command settings or spreadsheet format, manipulations and deletions, or spreadsheet style commands.

To use Undo you must first activate it with the /Options|Other|
Undo|Enable command. Since having Undo active slows down cer-
tain Quattro Pro operations, activate it only when needed.

Saving Your Spreadsheet

As you work in Quattro Pro, the data you enter into the spreadsheet is stored in the computer's memory. This memory is tempo-
rary, and it loses information when the system is turned off. To
store a spreadsheet permanently, you must save it to a disk file.
The first time you save a spreadsheet to disk, you must assign it
a name.

To save an unnamed spreadsheet:

1. Select /File|Save. Quattro Pro prompts you for a
    file name.

2. Enter a name 1–8 characters long, and press Enter.
    Restrictions on characters in file names are the same
    as for DOS file names. The WQ1 extension will be
    automatically added.

3. The spreadsheet file is saved to disk, and you are returned
    to READY mode. If the specified file name already exists
    on disk, you are offered three options: cancel the save
    operation, replace the old file with the new one, or back
    up the old file (with a BAK extension) and save the
    new one.

Once you have named a spreadsheet, you have two options for
saving it. You can save it under its present name, using the
/File|Save command, or you can save it under a new name with
the /File|Save As command. In either case, you will be prompted
to cancel, replace, or back up if the file already exists on disk.

You must save your spreadsheet before exiting Quattro Pro, or you
will lose all work done since the last save.

Retrieving a Spreadsheet

To use a spreadsheet that you have saved earlier, you must retrieve it from disk into the computer's memory. You can then continue working on it from where you left off before you saved it.

To retrieve a spreadsheet from disk:

1. If you are working on another spreadsheet, save it to disk.

2. Select /File|Retrieve. Quattro Pro displays a list of spreadsheet files in the current directory.

3. Highlight the name of the desired file using the arrow keys, and press Enter. With the mouse, click the desired file name. You can also type in the file name and press Enter.

4. The spreadsheet is read into memory and appears on the screen just as it was when you last saved it.

Changing the Data Directory

Quattro Pro's default is to save to and retrieve from the current directory (the current directory is listed on the File menu, next to the Directory command). If you are working with several projects, you may want to organize your files in different subdirectories on your disk (see your DOS manual for information on creating and using subdirectories). You can change the directory Quattro Pro uses for data either temporarily or permanently.

To change the Quattro Pro data directory temporarily:

1. Select /File|Directory

2. Quattro Pro displays the current directory. Type in the name of the new directory (including disk and/or path information, if needed) and press Enter.

3. The new directory will be in effect for the remainder of the work session (unless, of course, you change it again).

It will *not* remain in effect if you exit, then restart, Quattro Pro.

To change the Quattro Pro data directory permanently:

1. Select /Options|Startup|Directory. If a directory name is already displayed, press Esc to erase it.

2. Type in the name of the new directory (including disk and/or path information, if needed), then press Enter. The /Options|Startup|Directory menu will remain on the screen.

3. Select Quit to return to the /Options|Startup menu. Select Update|Quit to save your changes and return to READY mode.

4. The new directory will be in effect for the current and future work sessions.

One of Quattro Pro's most powerful features is its ability to use *formulas*. A formula performs a calculation based on values in other spreadsheet cells or in the formula itself. A cell that contains a formula displays the result of the calculation. For example, if you enter

What is a formula?

```
5+8
```

in a cell, it will display as 13. Similarly, if you enter

```
+A5+A6
```

in a cell, it will display the sum of the values in cells A5 and A6. A formula cell can itself be referenced by another formula, allowing you to create complex financial and mathematical models in your spreadsheet. Formulas are entered into cells and edited just like labels and numbers. The first character in a formula must be a digit or one of the following characters: ., +, −, (, @, #, or $. The uses of these characters are explained over the remainder of this step.

Most formulas reference other spreadsheet cells. This is done simply by including the cell address in the formula, as in the second example above. If a cell reference is the first element of a formula, precede it with a plus sign to tell Quattro Pro that the cell entry is a formula and not a label.

Referencing spreadsheet cells

Arithmetic Operators

The following symbols can be used in formulas to perform mathematical operations:

Operations in formulas

^   Exponentiation

−, +   Negative, positive

*, /   Multiplication, division

−, +   Subtraction, addition

Order of precedence

These operators are listed in order of *precedence,* i.e., the order in which operations are carried out. If a formula contains multiple operators, they are evaluated in order of precedence: exponentiation before division, division before addition, etc. Operators of equal precedence are evaluated from left to right. You can use parentheses in your formulas to force evaluation to proceed in a specific order. Sample formulas showing order of precedence are given in Table 4.1.

Formula	Result	Comments
4+3^2	13	Exponentiation is performed first.
4+3/2^2	4.75	Exponentiation is performed first, then division, then addition.
(4+3)^2	49	Parentheses force addition to be performed first.

Table 4.1: Sample formulas showing order of precedence

@functions

Quattro Pro's built-in formulas

An @function ("at" function) is a formula that is built into Quattro Pro. @functions are provided for several dozen commonly needed calculations, saving you the trouble of writing these formulas yourself. Each @function has a descriptive name that begins with the @ character. Most @functions require one or more arguments enclosed in parentheses following the function name. An argument is a value or label that the function operates on. For example, @SQRT(B5) calculates the square root of the value in cell B5; B5 is the argument.

The Quattro Pro @functions fall into eight categories:

- Mathematical functions perform calculations on values. For example, @LOG calculates the base 10 logarithm of a number.

- Statistical functions perform statistical calculations. For example, @VAR calculates the variance of a series of values.

- Financial functions perform financial calculations. For example, @FV calculates the future value of an annuity.

- String functions perform manipulations of text and spreadsheet labels. For example, @TRIM removes leading and trailing spaces from a label.

- Date and time functions are used with date and time serial numbers. For example, @TODAY returns the current date as a serial number.

- Database functions perform calculations on data in a Quattro Pro database (covered in Steps 16 and 17).

- Logical functions perform logical tests. @ISERR, for example, determines if a spreadsheet cell contains an error.

- Miscellaneous functions perform various tasks such as determining the amount of memory available.

@functions can be used alone or as components of complex formulas. An @function can even be used as the argument of another @function. For complete information on Quattro Pro's @functions, refer to the *@functions and Macros Guide*.

Formula Recalculation

When you first enter a formula into your spreadsheet, Quattro Pro automatically evaluates it and displays the answer. As you continue to work on the spreadsheet, Quattro Pro will recalculate formulas so they accurately reflect changes in spreadsheet data.

Recalculation options

There are three available recalculation modes:

- Background mode (the default) recalculates between keystrokes. No pause is needed for recalculation to occur.

- Automatic mode recalculates all affected formulas after each entry in the spreadsheet. There may be a noticeable pause after each entry as recalculation proceeds, particularly with large spreadsheets.

- Manual mode recalculates only when you press F9. In manual mode, the CALC indicator displays on the bottom line of the screen whenever the spreadsheet is not up-to-date.

Select /Options|Recalculation|Mode to change recalculation mode. Background mode is fine for most situations. Use Automatic mode when the spreadsheet must be completely updated after each entry is made and before the next entry is made. Use Manual mode for large spreadsheets that contain many formulas and need not be updated after each entry.

Step 5

Working with Blocks

Blocks are an important Quattro Pro concept used in many of the operations you'll learn in this book. If you are familiar with using blocks, many aspects of spreadsheet use will be much easier.

Defining a Block

A block is any contiguous, rectangular region of cells and can be as small as a single cell or as large as the entire spreadsheet. A block is defined by the addresses of the cells at diagonally opposite corners, usually the upper left and lower right corners. The two cell addresses are separated by two periods. For example, A2..C4 designates a block containing the cells A2, A3, A4, B2, B3, B4, C2, C3, and C4.

Many Quattro Pro operations, such as printing, assigning styles, and copying data, require that you define a block to be operated on. You can specify a block by typing in the addresses of its corner cells or by using the mouse or keyboard to actually point at the block on the screen.

Naming a Block

Quattro Pro lets you assign a name to a block. You can define as many named blocks as needed. Once a block has been assigned a name, you can refer to it by that name in many spreadsheet operations. This can be a great time-saver.

To assign a name to a block of cells:

1. If you are using the keyboard, move the cell selector to one corner of the block.

2. Select /Edit|Names|Create. If any names are already assigned to blocks, they are displayed. Since you want to assign a new block name, these can be ignored. Type in the new name and press Enter.

3. You are returned to the spreadsheet with the mode indicator displaying POINT. If you are using the keyboard, use the arrow keys to highlight the block of cells. If you are using the mouse, point at one corner, then drag to highlight the entire block. A highlighted block is shown in Figure 5.1.

4. Press Enter. The block name is assigned, and you are returned to READY mode.

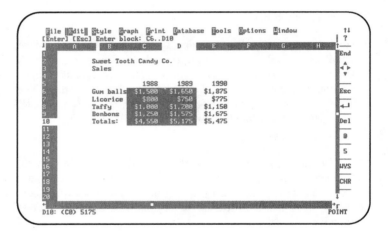

Figure 5.1: A highlighted block

At times you may need to redefine the block assigned to a particular name. This is also done with the /Edit|Names|Create command.

To redefine the block assigned to an existing name:

1. Select /Edit|Names|Create. A list of existing block names is displayed.

2. Highlight the desired name and press Enter, or click the name.

3. The spreadsheet is displayed with the name's current block assignment highlighted. If you simply want to expand or

contract the block assigned to the name, use the arrow keys to do so, then press Enter.

4. To define a totally new block, press Esc to erase the high-light. With the mouse, drag to highlight the new block, then press Enter. With the keyboard, move the cell selector to one corner of the new block, and press . (period) to anchor the corner. Use the arrow keys to highlight the new block and press Enter.

There are several other block commands you should know.

● To delete an existing block name, select /Edit|Names|
   Delete, then select the name to delete from the list that
   is displayed. Only the block name is deleted, not the
   data in the block.

Deleting a block name

● To delete all block names, select /Edit|Names|Reset|Yes.

● To display a list of all block names and their assignments,
   select /Edit|Names|Make Table. Next, highlight an empty
   spreadsheet region where you want the list to appear and
   press Enter. A list of block names and their assignments
   is displayed, as shown in Figure 5.2.

Displaying a list of block

```
 ile  dit  tyle  raph  rint  atabase  ools  ptions  indow        ↑↓
B13: 'SALES88                                                      | ?
J      A      B       C       D       E       F       G       H    |
1                                                                  End
2         Sweet Tooth Candy Co.                                    ▲
3         Sales                                                    ◄ ►
4                                                                  ▼
5                    1988     1989     1990
6         Gum balls  $1,500   $1,650   $1,875                      Esc
7         Licorice   $800     $750     $775
8         Taffy      $1,000   $1,200   $1,150                      ↵
9         Bonbons    $1,250   $1,575   $1,675
10        Totals:    $4,550   $5,175   $5,475                      Del
11
12                                                                 @
13        SALES88    C6..C9
14        SALES89    D6..D9                                        5
15        SALES90    E6..E9
16        TOTAL88    C10                                           ⋎YS
17        TOTAL89    D10
18        TOTAL90    E10                                           CHR
19
20                                                                 ↓
+                                                                  ⁺r
FIG5_1.WQ1   [1]                                                   READY
```

Figure 5.2: A list of block names and assignments

In the remainder of this step, and elsewhere in the book, you will be guided through procedures that require you to specify a block to operate on. Remember that there are three ways to specify a block:

- Type in the block's address.

- Type in the block's name (if one has been assigned).

- Highlight the block using either the mouse or the keyboard.

Manipulating Blocks

Much of the power of blocks comes from the ways that Quattro Pro lets you manipulate them. Blocks of data can be copied, moved, and erased. The procedures for these operations are the same no matter what types of data (labels, values, formulas, or a combination) the block contains, but you do have several options to consider when copying formulas. These options are covered in the final two sections of this step.

When you perform a Copy or Move operation, any data in the destination cells will be lost. However, you can use the Undo command (Alt-F5) to recover data if you make a mistake with Move, Copy, or Erase.

Moving a Block

The Move command lets you move a block of data from one spreadsheet location to another. After you move a block of data, the original cells are empty and the data exists only in the new location.

To move a block of data:

1. Select /Edit|Move.

2. Specify the source block of cells.

3. Specify the destination, which is a single cell marking the upper left corner of the destination block (which will have the same size as the source block). You can either type in the cell address, or move the cell pointer to it.

4. Press Enter, and data in the source block is moved to the destination block. If the destination block contains any existing data, it is overwritten by the new data.

Copying a Block

Copying a block of data is similar to moving except that after a copy operation, the data exists in both the old and new locations.

To copy a block of cells:

1. Select /Edit|Copy.

2. Specify the source block of cells.

3. Specify the destination, which is a single cell marking the upper left corner of the destination block (which will have the same size as the source block). You can either type in the cell address, or move the cell pointer to it.

4. Press Enter, and data in the source block is copied to the destination block. If the destination block contains any existing data, it is overwritten by the new data.

Copying can also be used to duplicate data in multiple spreadsheet cells. This can be particularly useful with formulas.

To duplicate data in multiple spreadsheet cells:

1. Select /Edit|Copy.

2. Specify as the source block the single cell containing the data item to be duplicated.

3. Specify the destination block that will contain the duplicated data, and press Enter.

4.   The data in the source cell is copied to every cell in the destination block.

Erasing a Block

To erase all data in a block, use the /Edit|Erase command. This command erases data but does not change cells' display format (display format is covered in Step 5).

To erase data in a block of cells:

1.   Select /Edit|Erase.

2.   Specify the block of cells to be erased, then press Enter.

Converting Formulas to Values

If your spreadsheet contains formulas whose values will never change, you can convert them to values. This is particularly useful with large spreadsheets. Converting formulas to values reduces recalculation time, reduces memory usage, and decreases disk file size.

To convert formulas to values:

1.   Select /Edit|Values, then specify the block of cells containing the formulas to be converted.

2.   Specify the destination. This is the single cell in the upper left corner of the region to receive the values.

3.   The formula results are copied, as values, to the destination cells. If the source and destination blocks are the same, the original formulas are overwritten by the values.

Absolute and Relative Cell References

Cell references in formulas are normally *relative,* meaning that they refer to a location relative to the cell containing the formula.

Thus, if you enter

+A2

in cell A3, it means "the value in the cell directly above this one." If you copy that formula to one or more other cells, the cell reference is adjusted to remain relative to its new location. If, for example, you copy the above formula from cell A3 to cell D10, it will change to

+D9

and will still mean "the cell directly above this one." For the majority of applications, relative cell references are appropriate.

At times, however, you may need a cell reference in a formula that is not relative—one that refers to the same specific spreadsheet cell no matter where you copy it. This is called an *absolute* cell reference. An absolute cell reference is created by including dollar signs before the column letter and/or row number. This is illustrated in Table 5.1.

Absolute cell references

Cell Reference	Comments
B1	Relative. Both row and column are adjusted when copied.
$B1	Column absolute. The row but not the column is adjusted when copied.
B$1	Row absolute. The column but not the row is adjusted when copied.
B1	Row and column absolute. Neither column nor row is adjusted when copied.

Table 5.1: Examples of absolute and relative cell references

When entering or editing a formula, you can type the dollar signs directly. You can also place the cursor on or immediately after a cell reference and press F4 one or more times to cycle through the various absolute/relative combinations.

Step 6

Formatting the Spreadsheet

30

The term *formatting* refers to changing the appearance of your spreadsheet. Changes in format do not affect the spreadsheet data, only the way data appears on the screen and in printouts. Proper use of formatting can greatly improve the readability and clarity of your spreadsheets, particularly with large, complex ones.

Aligning Cell Entries

Cell entries, both values and labels, can be displayed left-aligned, right-aligned, or centered in the cell. Quattro Pro's default is to display labels left-aligned and numbers and dates right-aligned. You can change data alignment to best suit your needs.

As you learned in Step 3, the alignment of labels is controlled by the label prefix character. You can change the alignment of a single label by editing the label (using the techniques learned in Step 3) to change its label prefix character. Remember, use ' for left-aligned, " for right-aligned, and ^ for centered.

Changing alignment

To change alignment for label and value entries in a block of cells, you use the /Style|Alignment command.

To change alignment in a block of cells:

1.   Select /Style|Alignment, or press Ctrl-A (the shortcut key for /Style|Alignment).

2.   Select the desired alignment: General for left-aligned labels and right-aligned numbers, or Left, Right, or Center to align both labels and numbers as indicated.

3.   Specify the block of cells to align and press Enter.

Formatting Number Cells

Quattro Pro offers a wide variety of numeric display formats. You can, for example, display numbers in currency format, with different numbers of decimal places, as percentages, and so on. The available numeric display formats are listed in Table 6.1.

Format	Examples	Description
Fixed	12.00 0.5600	Displays numbers with a specified number of decimal places and leading and trailing zeros.
Scientific	1.25E +03	Displays numbers in scientific notation.
Currency	$1,250.00 ($400.00)	Displays numbers with thousands separators, a dollar sign, and a specified number of decimal places. Negative numbers are displayed in parentheses.
, (Comma)	1,250.00 (1,000.00)	Displays numbers with thousands separators and two decimal places. Negative numbers are displayed in parentheses.
General	0.75 −1.02	Numbers are displayed as they are entered, with any trailing zeros deleted. If the number is too long for the current cell, it is rounded off (if fractional) or displayed in scientific notation.

Table 6.1: Numeric display formats

Format	*Examples*	*Description*
+/−	++++++ −−−−−	Numbers are converted into horizontal bar graphs, using + for positive values, − for negative values, and . for zero. Length of each bar is proportional to the value.
Percent	12% −1.05%	Numbers are displayed as a percentage, that is, multiplied by 100 and displayed with a specified number of decimal places and a trailing percent sign.
Date	4-Oct-89	Displays date/time serial numbers in several standard date and time formats.
Text	+A1/B2	Spreadsheet formulas are displayed as formulas rather than as their calculated values. Values are displayed in General format.
Hidden		Value and label entries are not displayed, but remain stored in the spreadsheet and will display on the status line when the cell selector is on the cell. Hidden entries can be edited, used in calculations, etc. Use Hidden format to hide sensitive data from prying eyes.
Reset		Returns numeric display format to the default format (which is initially General format).

Table 6.1: Numeric display formats (continued)

To change the numeric display format:

1. Select /Style|Numeric Format, or press the shortcut key Ctrl-F.

2. From the menu displayed, select the desired format. For some formats you must also enter the desired number of decimal places.

3. If you select Date, you must next select from several possible date/time formats.

4. Specify the block of cells you want the format applied to and press Enter.

When you assign a number format to a block of cells, it applies to all cells in the block. The display of blank and label cells in the block is not affected, but if a number is later placed in one of those cells it displays in the assigned format.

Changing Column Width

Quattro Pro columns can have 1–254 characters

Each column in a Quattro Pro spreadsheet starts out with a width of 9, meaning that 9 characters can be displayed. You can change the width to suit the data in the column; the allowed range of widths is 1–254. You can change the width of individual columns or of a block of adjacent columns.

To change the width of a single column:

1. If you are using the mouse, simply point at the letter at the top of the column and drag the column to the desired width.

2. If you are using the keyboard, move the cell selector to any cell in the column.

3. Select /Style|Column Width, or press the shortcut key Ctrl-W.

4. Enter the new column width, or use the ← and → keys to adjust the width visually. Then press Enter.

To change the width of a block of adjacent columns:

1. Select /Style|Block Widths.

2. Select Set Width to specify column width. Select Reset Width to reset column width to the default. Select Auto Width to have Quattro Pro automatically select a column width based on the length of data in the column.

3. Specify the columns to set by highlighting a block that spans the columns.

4. If you selected Set Width, enter the new column width or use the ← and → keys to adjust the width visually.

5. Press Enter.

You can use /Style|Block Width to set the width of a single column as well as a block of columns.

Changing the Format Defaults

Quattro Pro has defaults for label alignment, numeric format, and column width. These settings are used for all cells and columns that you haven't specifically formatted with one of the commands discussed in this step. You can change these defaults if you like.

To change the spreadsheet format defaults:

1. Select /Options|Format.

2. Select Numeric Format to change the default numeric format; then specify the desired format.

3. Select Align Labels to change the default label prefix; then select Left, Right, or Center to indicate where in the cell the label should be aligned.

Quattro Pro offers a number of formatting options that let you enhance the appearance of your spreadsheet. I call these *presentation-quality enhancements*. All of these enhancements appear on spreadsheet printouts.

WYSIWYG Mode

If you have an EGA or a VGA display, Quattro Pro offers WYSIWYG display mode. This acronym stands for "What You See Is What You Get." In this mode, the screen display accurately shows the effects of the spreadsheet enhancements discussed in this step. To switch to WYSIWYG mode, click the WYS button on the mouse palette or select /Options|Display Mode| WYSIWYG. While in WYSIWYG mode you can perform all spreadsheet operations. To return from WYSIWYG mode to normal character-based display mode, click the CHR button on the mouse palette, or select /Options| Display Mode|80x25.

Version 2 users: WYSIWYG mode is not available in release 2.0. Release 2.0 does have a graphics display mode, selected with the command /Options|Display Mode|Graphics. This mode, however, does not provide as much screen format information as WYSIWYG mode.

Drawing Lines

The Line Drawing option can be used to place vertical and horizontal lines between spreadsheet cells. These lines can be used to underline column headings, separate sections of data, clarify columns, and so on. The lines are not actually placed in spreadsheet rows or columns. Instead, Quattro Pro adds extra space between rows and columns for the lines. Note, however, that a vertical line decreases the width of the column to its left by one character.

Adding lines can improve clarity

Quattro Pro gives you several options for specifying where lines are to be placed within a block. Your choices are summarized below:

- All draws vertical and horizontal lines between and around all cells in the block.

- Outside draws lines around the outside of the block.

- Top or Bottom draws a single horizontal line above or below the block.

- Left or Right draws a single vertical line on the side of the block.

- Inside draws vertical and horizontal lines between cells within the block.

- Horizontal draws horizontal lines between cells within the block.

- Vertical draws vertical lines between cells within the block.

Occasion-
ally
different
line drawing
operations
yield
similar
results

Figure 7.1 shows the effects of several line drawing options. Note that under certain conditions, different line drawing operations have the same effect. For example, adding a line under row 5 has the same visual effect as adding a line above row 6.

To draw lines in a spreadsheet:

1. Select /Style|Line Drawing.

2. Specify the block of cells where you want lines drawn.

3. Next, specify the placement of lines within the block using the options listed above.

4. Select the type of line to use. You can choose from Single, Double, Thick, and None. Use None to remove lines from a block. The selected lines are drawn in the spreadsheet and you are returned to the Placement menu. The block selected in (2) remains in effect.

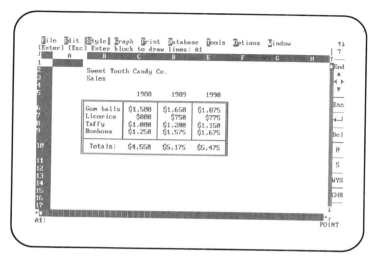

Figure 7.1: A spreadsheet enhanced with line drawing

5. Return to (3) if you want to add more lines to the block or delete or change existing lines. Otherwise, select Quit to return to READY mode.

When you add lines to a block of cells, the lines are "attached" to the individual cells. If you move or copy the data with /Edit|Copy or /Edit|Move, the cell's lines will be moved or copied as well.

Shading Areas

Quattro Pro lets you add background shading to a block of cells. There are two shading options that affect spreadsheet appearance when printed. With grey shading, the background of the cell is light grey and characters in the cell print in the normal black. With black shading, the background of the cell is black and characters in the cell print in white. If you have a color VGA monitor, both black and grey shading display on-screen as a stippled background in the portion of the cell not containing characters. The exact way shading displays and prints depends on your video hardware and monitor. A spreadsheet with shading is shown in Figure 7.2.

Quattro Pro offers light grey and black shading

To add shading to a block of cells:

1. Select /Style|Shading.

2. Select Grey or Black shading, or select None to remove shading from a block.

3. Specify the block to be shaded. The shading is displayed on the screen and will appear in any spreadsheet printouts. A screen preview of such a printout (based on the spreadsheet shown in Figure 7.2) is shown in Figure 7.3.

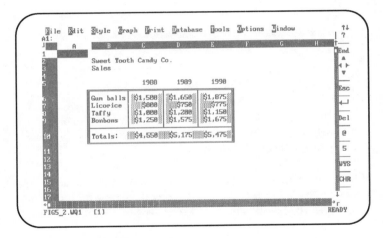

Figure 7.2: A spreadsheet with shading added

Using Fonts

You can use up to eight fonts in a single spreadsheet

Quattro Pro is supplied with a large number of fonts. The number available to you depends on the fonts that were generated during the installation process (see Step 1). At any time, up to eight of the available fonts can be used in a Quattro Pro spreadsheet.

Fonts are assigned to spreadsheet cells in the same manner as numeric formats. You will not see the different fonts displayed

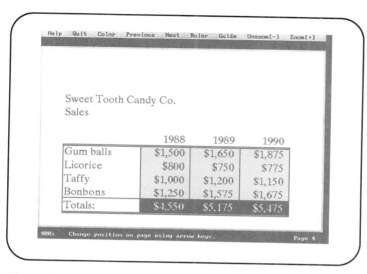

Figure 7.3: Screen preview of the spreadsheet in Figure 7.2

on the screen (except in a screen preview, covered in Step 8), but you will see them when printing your spreadsheet. Figure 7.4 shows a screen preview of a spreadsheet printed with several different fonts.

To change the font for a block of cells:

1. Select /Style|Font. Quattro Pro displays a list of the eight currently available fonts.

2. Select the desired font.

3. Specify the block to be printed in the selected font.

Different fonts do not display in the spreadsheet, but you can determine which font a cell has assigned to it. Move the cell selector to the cell and look at the input line. If any font other than the default has been assigned to that cell, it will display in the input line as [F*n*], where *n* is the font number.

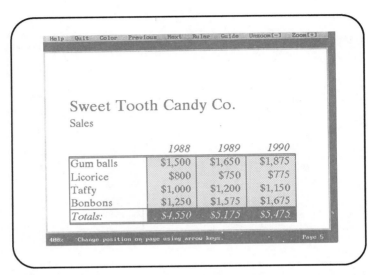

Figure 7.4: Screen preview of a spreadsheet printed using several different fonts

Bullets

Use bullets to empha- size items in a list

A *bullet* is a symbol used to set off items in a list. Quattro Pro has seven different bullet styles you can use in your printouts. To print a bullet, you include a bullet code in the corresponding label cell (bullets cannot be included in value cells). The code is \bullet *n*\, where *n* is a number from 0–6 specifying the bullet to use. Bullets do not display on the screen; they appear only in screen previews and in printouts.

A spreadsheet with bullet codes is shown in Figure 7.5 and the corresponding screen preview in Figure 7.6.

If the bullet code is the first entry in a cell, remember to enter a label prefix character before the first backslash.

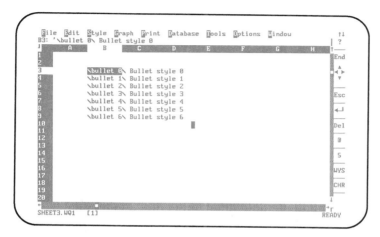

Figure 7.5: A spreadsheet containing bullet codes

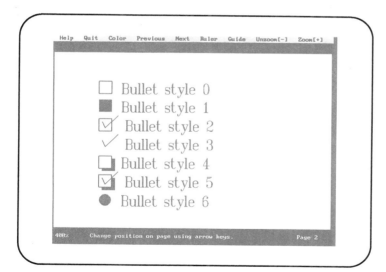

Figure 7.6: Screen preview of the spreadsheet in Figure 7.5

If your computer has a printer hooked up to it, you can create printouts of information in your spreadsheet. Printing graphs is a separate topic and will be covered in Step 12.

Specifying Print Destination

When printing data from a Quattro Pro spreadsheet, you have several options as to the print destination. This choice is made on the /Print|Destination menu, shown in Figure 8.1.

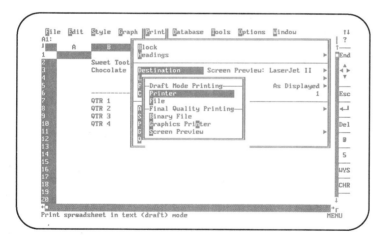

Figure 8.1: The /Print|Destination menu

Under Draft Mode Printing you have two options:

Draft mode printing

- Printer sends output to the default printer in text mode. Text mode means that special effects, such as line drawing and shading, will not be reproduced. Use this destination for a quick printout showing the layout of your data on the page.

- File sends text mode output to an ASCII disk file (whose name you specify). Use File to save spreadsheet data in a form that can be imported into word processors and other programs.

Final quality printing

Under Final Quality Printing you have three options:

- Graphics Printer sends output to the default graphics printer. All special effects in your worksheet, including shading, fonts, and inserted graphs, will be reproduced.

- Screen Preview displays a screen image showing what the final printed output will look like. More details on Screen Preview are given later in this step.

- Binary File creates a disk file containing the same information that would have been sent to the printer had you selected Graphics Printer. This file will include your data as well as all special printer control codes. If you later send this file to the printer you will get the same printout as if you had printed directly to the graphics printer from Quattro Pro.

Printing

You can print as much or little spreadsheet data as you like. A printout can be a single cell, or an entire spreadsheet that requires multiple pages to print. When a printout is too large to fit on one page, Quattro Pro automatically breaks it into multiple pages.

To print spreadsheet data:

1. Select /Print|Destination, and choose a print destination as described above. After selecting your destination you are returned to the /Print menu.

Specifying data to print

2. Select Block, then specify the block of cells to print. If a block is already specified, press Enter to accept it or Esc to cancel it. Then specify a new block.

3. If necessary, select Headings, Layout, or Format to set various print options (explained below).

4. If you selected /Print|Destination|Printer or /Print|Destination|Graphics Printer, make sure your printer is turned on and is online.

5. If you are using a dot-matrix printer, make sure the paper is aligned at the top of a page before turning it on. Select Adjust Printer|Align to tell Quattro Pro that it's at the top of a page.

6. Select Spreadsheet Print, and printing will begin. Quattro Pro will display a message that printing is in progress. You can press Ctrl-Break to interrupt printing.

If an error occurs during printing (if your printer is out of paper, for example), an error message is displayed on the screen along with two choices. You can correct the problem and then select Continue, or you can select Abort to cancel printing.

Print Options

Quattro Pro's print options let you enhance your printed reports in various ways. Although a complete treatment of these options is beyond the scope of this book, you will find brief descriptions of the various options below; and you can refer to your Quattro Pro documentation for further information.

You can use the /Print menu's Headings command to designate worksheet columns and/or rows as headings to be printed at the top or left of every printed page. Use the Headings command to ensure that explanatory column and row labels appear on every page of multipage reports.

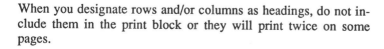

When you designate rows and/or columns as headings, do not include them in the print block or they will print twice on some pages.

The /Print menu's Format command controls the format of the printout. There are two options to choose from. The As Displayed

*Print
format
options*

option, the default, prints the spreadsheet as it appears on screen. The Cell-Formulas option prints a list of all worksheet cells, one to a line, with the contents of each cell displayed as it was entered. Formulas print as formulas, not as the calculated result. Use Cell-Formulas format when debugging a spreadsheet.

The Layout command on the /Print menu offers a number of choices that affect the way data appears on the printed page. Each of these is described briefly below. Remember, you can use the Screen Preview to check the effects of Layout options before you print to a printer.

*Printing
headers
and footers*

- Select Layout|Header or Layout|Footer to enter text that will print at the top or bottom of each page.

- Select Break Pages to determine whether Quattro Pro will print with page breaks. The default is Yes. Select No when printing to an ASCII disk file.

*Changing
the
margins*

- Select Layout|Margins to specify the page length and the top, bottom, left, and right page margins. Set the top and bottom margins to 0 when printing to an ASCII file that will be imported into a word processor.

- Select Layout|Dimensions to change the units used for page measurements. The default is for vertical distance to be measured in lines, horizontal distance to be measured in characters. The other available options are Inches and Centimeters.

- Select Layout|Orientation to determine the print orientation: Portrait (the default) or Landscape (Landscape orientation prints data rotated 90° on the page, parallel to the long edge of the paper).

- Select Layout|Setup String to enter special printer commands that will be sent to your printer at the start of each print job.

- Select Layout|Reset to reset some or all print settings to their default values.

- Select Layout|Update to make the current print settings the defaults.

Screen Preview

If you select /Print|Destination|Screen Preview, Quattro Pro will display a screen image showing what the final printout will look like. You must have a graphics-capable video system to use Screen Preview. Screen Preview lets you fine-tune your printed reports without wasting time and paper by printing lots of test runs. The Screen Preview screen is shown in Figure 8.2.

Previewing your printout

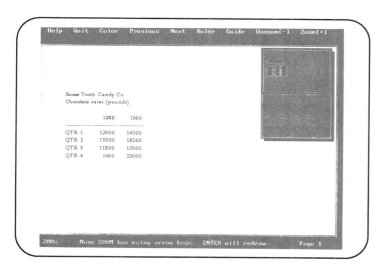

Figure 8.2: The Screen Preview screen

The status line at the bottom of the screen gives the zoom level. A zoom level of 100% displays an entire page, and zoom levels greater than 100% display part of a page. When you are viewing part of a page, the guide in the upper right corner of the screen shows the whole page in miniature, with an outline around the portion of the page being displayed in the main portion of the screen. Use the arrow keys to move the zoom box, and press Enter to display the newly selected region.

When you display a screen preview, a menu across the top of the screen offers several commands. The commands, their keystrokes, and their functions are summarized in the list below.

- /Help or F1 displays Help on Screen Preview.

- /Color switches between different sets of display colors.

- /Previous or PgUp displays the previous page (applicable to multipage printouts only).

- /Next or PgDn displays the next page (applicable to multipage printouts only).

- Home and End display the top or bottom of a zoomed page, respectively.

- /Ruler toggles the display of a one-inch grid.

- /Guide toggles display of the miniature page guide visible when you are viewing a zoomed page. You can also press Ins to display the guide or Del to hide it.

- /Unzoom[−] reduces the zoom factor. Pressing the − key on the keypad yields the same result.

- /Zoom[+] increases the zoom factor. You can also press the + key on the keypad for the same effect.

- /Quit or Esc exits Screen Preview and returns you to

Much of Quattro Pro's power comes from its ability to quickly and easily create graphs of your worksheet data. A graph can often reveal trends in data that are not obvious from viewing the numbers alone.

Graph Types

Quattro Pro offers 14 different types, or styles, of graphs:

- Line, Area, and XY graphs display data values as lines and/or points.

- Bar, Stacked Bar, Rotated Bar, and Column graphs display data values as vertical or horizontal bars.

- Pie graphs display data values as segments of a circle.

- High-Low graphs are used to display stock market data.

- Text graphs do not display data, but use Quattro Pro's graph annotation features to create lists, organization charts, etc.

- There are four 3-dimensional graph types (Bar, Ribbon, Step, and Area) that display data values in a three dimensional perspective.

Each different graph type is designed for displaying particular kinds of data. For the most part, however, the same fundamentals apply to all of Quattro Pro's graph types.

Graph Basics

Figure 9.1 shows some spreadsheet data, and Figure 9.2 shows a graph created from that data. This is a bar graph, but most of its components are found in the other graph types as well. All graph types use data that is organized into *data series*. A data series is a block of spreadsheet data that is displayed in the graph.

Elements of a graph

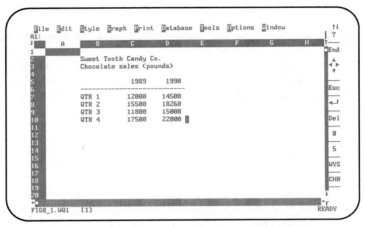

Figure 9.1: Sample spreadsheet data graphed in Figure 9.2

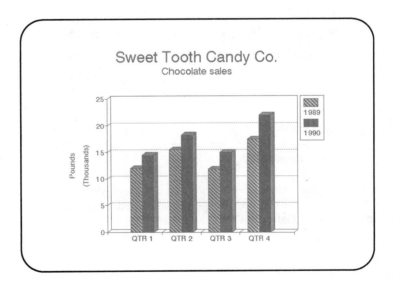

Figure 9.2: Bar graph of the data in Figure 9.1

All graph types except Pie and Text display data on two axes: the X axis, which runs horizontally, and the Y axis, which runs vertically. The X axis displays a single data series that contains values (for XY graphs) or labels (for all other graph types). The Y axis displays one or more data series containing values. Pie and Column graphs can display only a single Y data series; all other types can display as many as six Y data series.

The bar graph in Figure 9.2 is displaying one X data series and two Y data series. In the spreadsheet in Figure 9.1, the block B7..B10 is the X data series, C7..C10 is the first Y data series, and D7..D10 is the second Y data series.

Creating a Graph

There are four basic steps to creating and displaying a graph:

1.   Choose a graph type.

2.   Specify the X data series and one or more Y data series.

3.   Add titles and a legend, if desired.

4.   View the graph.

Choosing a Graph Type

To choose a graph type, select /Graph|Graph Type. A submenu is displayed listing the available types. If you do not specify a graph type, the default is Stacked Bar. The name of the currently selected type is displayed next to the Graph Type entry on the /Graph menu.

Specifying Data Series

To specify data series, select Series from the /Graph menu. The next submenu lists the Y series, numbered 1 through 6, and the X series. Select the series, then specify the block of data to be graphed. Remember, you can specify a block by entering its cell addresses, by pointing, or by using an assigned block name. Repeat the process for each series; you must specify an X series and at least one Y series. As you specify series, the addresses of the selected blocks are displayed on the /Graph|Series menu. When all series have been specified, select Quit to return to the /Graph menu.

Adding Titles and Legend

You can add titles and a legend to your graph to increase its impact and clarify its meaning. To do so, select Text from the /Graph menu. The next submenu offers the following choices:

- 1st Line is the main graph title, displayed at the top.

- 2nd Line is the secondary graph title, displayed under the main title.

- X-Title is the X-axis title.

- Y-Title is the Y-axis title.

- Secondary Y-Axis is the title of the optional secondary Y axis.

- Legends assigns descriptive text for the various Y data series.

- Font specifies the font to use for the various titles and legends.

When entering a title or legend, you can type in the text directly. You can also enter a backslash (\) followed by the address of a spreadsheet cell containing a label to be used as the title or legend.

Viewing the Graph

To view the currently defined graph, select View from the /Graph menu or press F10 from READY mode. When you are done looking at the graph, press any key to return to the spreadsheet.

Naming Graphs

After defining a graph you can assign a name to it. Once a graph is named you can recall it without having to reenter all of its specifications. A Quattro Pro worksheet can contain an unlimited number of named graphs. Be sure to save your spreadsheet after assigning graph names.

To assign a name to the current graph:

1. Select /Graph|Name|Create.

2. Type in the name you want assigned to the current graph and press Enter. The name can be up to 15 characters long.

You can use the other commands on the /Graph|Name menu as follows:

*   Select Display to view a named graph. The graph you select becomes the current graph.

*   Select Erase to delete a named graph.

*   Select Reset to delete all named graphs.

*   Select Slide to create a slide show of named graphs.

*   Select Graph Copy to copy a named graph to another spreadsheet.

To have Quattro Pro automatically save any changes you make to a named graph, select /Graph|Name|Autosave Edits|Yes. *Version 2 users:* This command is not available.

Three-Dimensional Graphs

Quattro Pro offers four 3-dimensional (3-D) graph types: Bar, Ribbon, Step, and Area. These graph types use a three-dimensional perspective, placing the different Y data series at different "depths" in the graph. To create a 3-D graph, select /Graph|Graph Type|3-D Graphs, then choose the desired type from the list presented. Other aspects of creating 3-D graphs, such as specifying data series, are the same as for other graph types. Figure 9.3 shows the data from Figure 9.2 displayed as a 3-D bar graph.

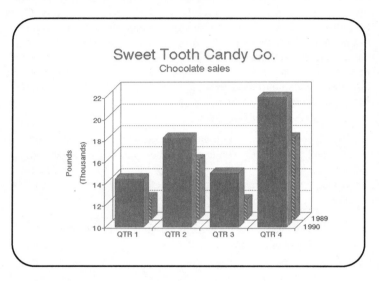

Figure 9.3: A 3-dimensional bar graph

Step 9 showed you how to create a graph that relies on the Quattro Pro defaults for many of its features. This will be fine for many situations, but you may sometimes want to customize a graph to meet a particular need. You can customize individual data series, the graph axes, or the overall graph. This step covers Quattro Pro's most commonly used graph customizations.

Customizing Data Series

When you customize a data series, you modify the way that the series is displayed in the graph.

Changing Color and Fill Pattern

You can change the color and/or fill pattern used for the Y data series. Color applies to all graph types, while fill pattern only applies to such types as bar and pie.

To change the color or fill pattern used to display a data series:

1. Select /Graph|Customize Series, then select Colors or Fill Patterns. A list of the six Y data series is displayed along with the color or fill pattern currently assigned to each series.

2. Select the data series you want to change. A list of the available color or fill options is displayed.

3. Select the desired color or fill pattern.

4. Repeat (2) and (3) until all desired series have been changed, then select Quit or press Escape.

Changing Line and Marker Style

Line graphs and XY graphs use markers and lines to display data series. The default is for both markers and lines to be used: a marker, or symbol, is displayed at each data point, and lines are drawn between the markers. You can change the type of marker and line used for a data series, and specify the format (i.e., whether lines, markers, or both are displayed). Line types include solid, dashed, and dotted. Marker types include squares, triangles, and asterisks.

To change marker, line style, or format for a data series in a Line or XY graph:

1. Select /Graph|Customize Series, then select Line Styles, Markers, or Format. A list of the six Y data series is displayed along with the line style, marker, or format currently assigned to each series.

2. Select the data series you want to change. A list of the available line style, marker, or format options is displayed.

3. Select the desired line style, marker, or format.

4. Repeat (2) and (3) until all desired series have been changed, then select Quit.

Changing Bar Width

You can change the width of the bars displayed in bar, stacked bar, and rotated bar graphs. Bar width is expressed as a percentage of the total distance between bars. The default value is 60% and the allowable range is 20–90%, with lower values giving thinner bars. The set bar width applies to all data series. To change the bar width, select /Graph|Customize Series|Bar Width, and enter the new bar width.

Adding Interior Labels

An interior label is a text label associated with a particular data point. For example, in Figure 10.1, the label "Best yet!" is an interior

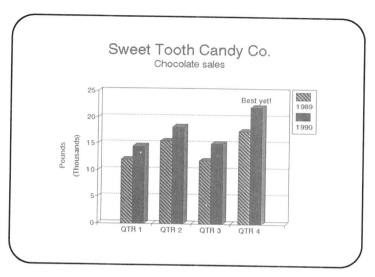

Figure 10.1: A graph with an interior label added

label. Use interior labels to clarify data or emphasize certain points on the graph.

To add interior labels to a graph:

1. Create the graph, then return to READY mode.

2. Locate an empty spreadsheet block for the labels. The block should contain one cell for each value in the data series (e.g., if the data series contains four values, as do the two Y series in Figure 10.1, your block should contain four cells). Enter the desired labels or values in the block, leaving blank cells for those data points you don't want labeled.

3. Select /Graph|Customize Series|Interior Labels; then select the data series to be labeled. Next, specify the block containing the labels.

4. Finally, select the position the labels will have relative to their data point markers: Center, Left, Above, Right, or Below. Select None to remove interior labels from

a series. With bar graphs, labels are always displayed above the data point.

Customizing the Entire Graph

Certain customization features affect the entire graph. These commands are accessed by selecting the /Graph|Overall command. From the next submenu, you have several choices:

- Select Grid to modify the color, style, or pattern of the graph's background grid lines.

- Select Outlines to customize the frames displayed around titles, legends, and the graph.

- Select Background Color to change the graph's background color.

- Select Three-D to determine whether the graph is displayed with a three-dimensional perspective (applies only to certain graph types).

- Select Color/B&W to determine whether the graph is displayed in color or monochrome.

Saving and Resetting Graph Customizations

After customizing a graph you can reset some or all graph features to their original default values. This is done with the Graph| Customize Series|Reset command. You can also save the changed settings as the new defaults by selecting /Graph|Customize Series| Update. Before resetting graph features, be sure you are finished with the graph or have assigned it a name.

Annotation is the process of adding descriptive elements to a graph. With Quattro Pro's Graph Annotator, you can add text to a graph, insert arrows and lines, draw special symbols or logos, resize graph elements, and more. When you have selected the Text graph type, the Annotator is used to create flow charts, bulleted lists, and other textual graphic aids. Figure 11.1 shows a graph with several annotations added.

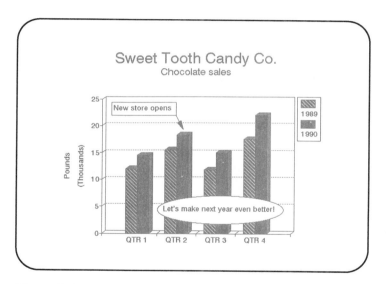

Figure 11.1: A graph with several annotations

Every Quattro Pro graph consists of a number of *elements*. As defined in the spreadsheet, a graph contains three elements: the titles, the legend, and the body of the graph. Using the Annotator, you can perform two main actions:

- Add new elements to the graph.
- Modify existing elements.

The Quattro Pro Annotator is a complex and full-featured graphics tool, and a full description of its abilities is beyond the scope of this book. This step will describe the basics of Annotator use.

The Annotator Screen

To activate the Annotator, either select /Graph|Annotate from READY mode or press / while viewing a graph. The Annotator screen is displayed, with the current graph in the draw area. The Annotator screen is shown in Figure 11.2.

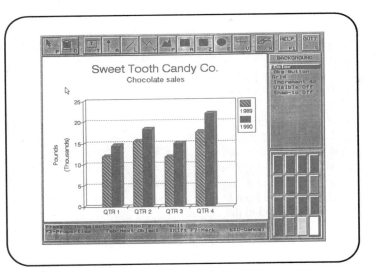

Figure 11.2: The Annotator screen

The Annotator screen has five main sections:

- The *draw area* displays the current graph. You work in the draw area to annotate a graph.

- The *toolbox,* displayed along the top of the screen, contains icons for the various Annotator tools. Select the proper tool to add elements to the graph or to perform other actions.

- The *property sheet,* at the upper right side of the screen, displays information about the properties of the currently selected graph element or tool.

- The *gallery,* at the lower right corner of the screen, displays options available for the currently selected element or tool.

- The *status box,* at the bottom of the screen, displays menu command descriptions, shortcut keys, and instructions.

If you select a graph element or tool, those element properties that can be modified are listed in the property sheet. For example, if you select the Graph Legend element, you can modify the Color and Font of the legend text, and the Color and Type of the legend box. Therefore, these four properties will be listed on the property sheet. Similarly, if you select the Line tool from the toolbox section (used to add lines to the graph), the modifiable properties Color and Style will be listed on the property sheet.

The property sheet and gallery

To activate the property sheet, press F3. You can then use the ↑ and ↓ keys to select the property you wish to change. The available options for the selected property will be displayed in the gallery, and you can select one with the arrow keys or the mouse. For example, Figure 11.3 shows the Annotator screen with the Line tool active and the Line Style property selected. The available line styles are displayed in the gallery.

Moving Around the Annotator Screen

The Annotator can be used with the keyboard alone, but a mouse makes things much easier. The Annotator cursor moves with the mouse or with the cursor pad keys. To move the cursor using the keyboard:

- Press the arrow keys to move the cursor vertically or horizontally.

- Press Home, PgUp, PgDn, or End to move the cursor diagonally.

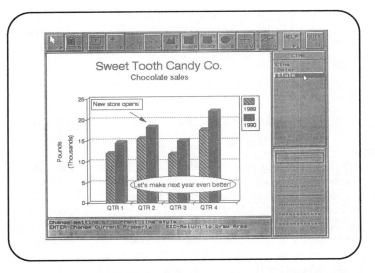

Figure 11.3: The gallery displays options for the currently selected property

- Hold down the Shift key while pressing the above keys to move the cursor in larger steps.

The cursor is used to position elements in the draw area. If you're using a mouse, it can also be used to select Annotator commands.

Adding Elements to a Graph

To add an element to a graph, you must first select the appropriate tool from the toolbox, then place the element in the graph. The tools that add elements are located in the central section of the toolbox. Each tool is identified by an icon and a letter.

- Text (T) adds text, which can be enclosed in a box if desired.

- Arrow (A) adds arrows.

- Line (L) draws straight lines.

- Polyline (Y) draws multiple-segment lines.

- Polygon (F) creates an irregular polygon.

- Rectangle (R) creates a rectangle.

- Rounded rectangle (Z) draws a rectangle with rounded corners.

- Ellipse (E) draws an ellipse or a circle.

- Vertical/Horizontal (V) draws vertical or horizontal lines.

To add an element to a graph:

1. Select the desired tool by clicking with the mouse or pressing / followed by the tool's letter.

2. Using the mouse or the keyboard, move the cursor to the location where you want the element positioned.

3. To use the Text tool, use the mouse or the keyboard to position the cursor at the location you want the text to start. Then type in the desired text and press Enter.

4. To use other tools: If you are using the mouse, press and hold the mouse button, drag the element to the desired size, and release the button. If you are using the keyboard, press and release the . (period) key, use the cursor keys to expand the element to the desired size, and press Enter.

Modifying Existing Graph Elements

Existing graph elements are modified using the Pick tool, identified by the letter *P* and located at the far left of the toolbox. When the Pick tool is active, you can select any single graph element and modify its position or properties, or you can delete it.

To modify the properties of a graph element:

1. Select the Pick tool by clicking it with the mouse or pressing **/P**.

2. Select a graph element by clicking it with the mouse. If you are using the keyboard, press Tab until the desired object is selected. Small boxes called *handles* are displayed around the perimeter of the selected object. For example, in Figure 11.4 the graph title is selected.

3. The element's properties will be displayed in the property sheet. Select the property you want to change by clicking it with the mouse or by pressing F3, using the arrow keys to highlight the property, and pressing Enter. The available property selections will be displayed in the gallery or in a dialog box. Use the keyboard or mouse to make a selection. The new property will be displayed in the draw area immediately.

To delete an element, simply select it and press Del.

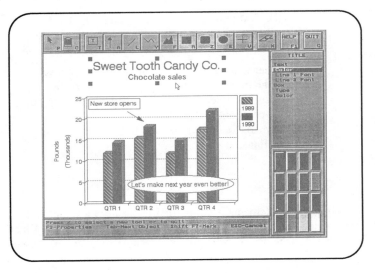

Figure 11.4: Handles indicate that the graph title is the selected element

To change the position or size of a graph element:

1. Select the Pick tool, then select the desired graph element as described above.

2. To move the element with the mouse, drag its outline to the new location, then release the mouse button. To move it with the keyboard, use the cursor pad keys to move the outline to the new position, then press Enter.

3. To resize an element with the mouse, point at one of its handles, then drag the element's outline to the desired size and release the mouse button. If you are using the keyboard, press . (period) one or more times until the correct handle is displayed. Next, use the cursor pad keys to stretch the element's outline to the desired size and press Enter.

Aligning Graph Objects

The Annotator lets you align selected objects in the graph. To do so, select the objects to be aligned using the procedures described in the exercise above. When two or more objects are selected, the Group menu is displayed. Select Align from the menu, then select the desired alignment from the choices that are displayed. For example, select Left Sides to align the left sides of all of the objects with the left edge of the leftmost object.

Printing Graphs

If you have a graphics-capable printer attached to your system, you can create printouts of your Quattro Pro graphs. The procedure for printing graphs is similar in some respects to printing spreadsheet data. All graph printing operations are accessed via the Graph Print command on the Graph menu.

Print Destination

When printing a graph you have three choices of destination:

- Graphics Printer sends the graph directly to your printer.

- File creates a disk file containing the same information that would have been sent to the printer had you selected Graphics Printer. This file will include all graph printing commands. If you send this file to the printer later, you will get the same graph printout as if you had printed directly to the graphics printer.

- Screen Preview displays an on-screen image of what the final printed graph will look like. Details on using Screen Preview were given in Step 8.

If you are using a dot-matrix printer, set the paper to the top of a page and select /Print|Adjust Printer|Align|Quit before printing your first graph.

Selecting the Graph to Print

Quattro Pro's default is to print the current graph, that is, the one that is displayed if you press F10 in READY or MENU mode. You can print a named graph using the Name command on the /Print|Graph Print menu.

To print a graph:

1. Select /Print|Graph Print|Destination and choose the desired destination for the printout. If the destination is your graphics printer, make sure your printer is turned on and is online.

2. To print the current graph, simply select Go. To print a named graph, select Name, specify the name of the graph to print, and select Go.

During printing, Quattro Pro displays screen messages informing you of the progress of the print session. If an error occurs (e.g., running out of paper), an error message displays. You then have the choice of aborting the print session or correcting the problem and continuing.

Graph Layout Options

Quattro Pro's graph layout options allow you to control the size, position, and orientation of the printed graph. To change layout, select /Print|Graph Print|Layout. A submenu offers you the following choices:

- Left Edge controls the margin between the left edge of the paper and the left edge of the graph.

- Top Edge controls the margin between the top edge of the paper and the top of the graph.

- Height controls the height of the graph.

- Width controls the width of the graph.

- Dimensions can be set to either inches or centimeters.

- Orientation can be either Portrait or Landscape.

- 4:3 Aspect Ratio refers to the graph's width:height ratio. If set to Yes, graphs are always printed with a 4:3 aspect ratio, which preserves the width:height dimensions of text and other elements in their proper proportion. If set to No, the exact Width and Height settings are used.

- Reset returns all graph layout settings to the default values.

- Update saves the current graph layout settings as the new defaults.

Quattro Pro's defaults are Left and Top Edges of 0, Width of 8, and Height of 6 (default dimensions are expressed in inches). The right and bottom margins depend on paper size, edge settings, and graph size. For example, with 8½-inch wide paper, a Left Edge setting of 1 inch and a Width setting of 4 inches will give a right margin of 3½ inches.

Default layout options

For the largest possible graph size, select Landscape orientation, Left and Top edges of 0, Width of 11 inches, and set 4:3 Aspect to Yes.

Inserting Graphs in the Spreadsheet

Quattro Pro lets you insert graphs into the spreadsheet. An inserted graph can display on the screen and be printed along with your spreadsheet data. When displayed on the screen, an inserted graph changes to reflect changes in data, allowing you to see the effects of spreadsheet manipulations immediately. Printing inserted graphs lets you create reports that include data and graphs on the same page. Figure 12.1 shows a spreadsheet with an inserted graph.

To insert a graph in the spreadsheet:

1. Select /Graph|Insert, then select either a named graph or the current graph.

2. Specify the block of spreadsheet cells where the graph is to be placed, then select Quit. You should select empty cells.

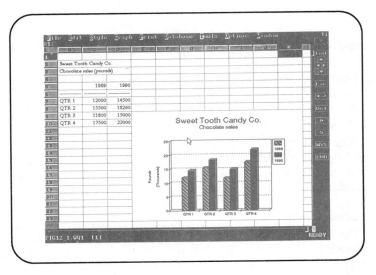

Figure 12.1: A spreadsheet with an inserted graph

3. In the character screen display mode, the graph block will display as highlighted cells. To display the actual graph, you must switch to WYSIWYG display mode by selecting /Options|Display Mode|WYSIWYG. This is possible only if you have an EGA or VGA display.

Version 2 users: WYSIWYG mode is not available. To view an inserted graph, switch to graphics display mode by selecting /Options|Display Mode|Graphics (possible only with an EGA or VGA adapter).

To print an inserted graph, simply include it in the block of cells specified with the /Print|Block command.

Because most spreadsheets are much too large to view all at once, the Quattro Pro screen provides a window onto your spreadsheet. Normally, the window displays a single region of 20 rows and 8 columns. You can scroll around the spreadsheet to view different regions. Quattro Pro also lets you simultaneously view two different regions of the spreadsheet, and offers several other spreadsheet viewing options to make your work easier.

Multiple Panes

The Quattro Pro window can be split vertically or horizontally into two *panes*. Each pane displays a different region of the same spreadsheet. You can perform all spreadsheet activities with a split window, including copying and moving data between panes. Changes made in either pane become part of the spreadsheet. Figure 13.1 shows a spreadsheet window split into two vertical panes.

Viewing two parts of a spread-sheet

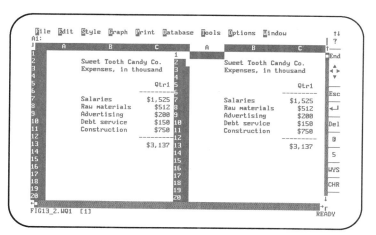

Figure 13.1: A spreadsheet window split into two vertical panes

To split a window into two panes:

1. Move the cell selector to the row (for a horizontal split) or column (for a vertical split) where you want the split to be placed.

2. Select /Window|Options and select either Horizontal or Vertical. The window will be split at the location of the cell selector.

3. To move the cell selector between panes, click the desired pane with the mouse or press F6.

4. To return to a single-window display, select /Window| Options|Clear.

Synchronizing Panes

When you first split a window, the two panes are synchronized. This means that scrolling in one pane (the one containing the cell selector) causes the other pane to scroll as well. Synchronization works only in the same direction the window was split:

- If the window is split vertically, only vertical scrolling is synchronized; the two panes always display the same rows.

- If the window is split horizontally, only horizontal scrolling is synchronized; the two panes always display the same columns.

You must unsynchronize the panes to view spreadsheet regions that do not share rows or columns. To unsynchronize the panes, select /Window|Options|Unsynch. To turn synchronization back on, select /Window|Options|Synch.

When a window is split into panes, you can modify certain aspects of one pane's appearance without affecting the other pane. These settings include column width (both local and global) and the global setting for cell format.

Row and Column Titles

Locking titles on the screen

Many spreadsheet applications include identifying titles at the top of each column and/or at the left of each row of data. If the rows and columns are long, the titles may scroll off the screen at times, making it difficult to identify the data you are working with. You can lock row and column titles in the window so they remain visible no matter where you scroll to. If you lock horizontal titles, one or more rows will be locked in place at the top edge of the window. If you lock vertical titles, one or more columns will be locked in place at the left edge of the window. You can lock both vertical and horizontal titles at the same time.

To lock titles on the screen:

1. For horizontal titles, move the cell selector to any cell in the row just below the lowest title row. For example, to lock rows 1 and 2 as titles, move the cell selector to row 3. For vertical titles, move the cell selector to the column just to the right of the title column(s).

2. Select / Window|Options|Locked Titles, then select Vertical, Horizontal, or Both. To unlock titles, select / Window|Options|Locked Titles|Clear.

If you have a color display, the locked titles will be displayed in a different color from other spreadsheet cells. You cannot move the cell selector into a locked row or column.

Spreadsheet Border Display

Control-ling border display

The spreadsheet border consists of the column letters and row numbers that are normally displayed at the top and left edges of the window. Most of the time you need these displayed to help you navigate the spreadsheet; however, they can be hidden, which permits slightly more data to be displayed on the screen. Figure 13.2 shows a spreadsheet with the row and column borders hidden. To hide the borders, select /Window|Options|Row & Col Borders|Hide. Select /Window|Options|Row & Col Borders|Display to restore the borders.

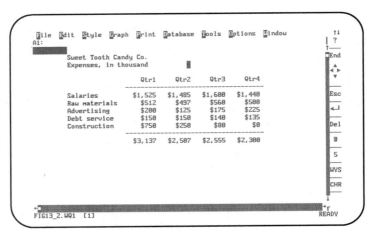

Figure 13.2: A spreadsheet with row and column borders hidden

Map View

Map View is a special display mode that gives you an overall picture of the structure of your spreadsheet. To activate map view, select /Window|Options|Map View|Yes. The display changes so that each cell is one character wide. Each occupied cell displays a single character code indicating its contents, as shown below (linked formulas are covered in Step 15):

l   label

n   value

+   formula

—   linked formula

c   circular formula

g   inserted graph

In Map View you see a region of the spreadsheet 72 columns wide. You can move the cell pointer to any cell, and the input line will display the cell's contents. You can enter new data and edit existing data while in Map View. To turn off Map View, select /Window|Options|Map View|No.

Step 14

Multiple Spreadsheets

45

Quattro Pro lets you work on multiple spreadsheets simultaneously. Each spreadsheet is contained in its own screen window, which may or may not be visible at any particular time. You can view multiple spreadsheets one at a time, full-screen, displaying other windows as needed; or you can resize windows to display more than one spreadsheet at the same time. When multiple spreadsheets are open, you can copy and move data and establish links between them. You can have as many as 32 spreadsheets open at one time.

Opening a New Spreadsheet Window

When you start Quattro Pro, you are presented with a single blank spreadsheet window. You can either enter data into the window or read an existing spreadsheet into the window from disk with the /File|Retrieve command. To open a new spreadsheet window use either the /File|New or the /File|Open command:

- /File|New opens a new, blank spreadsheet window with the name SHEETn, where n depends on the number of spreadsheets open. The new window is displayed full-screen. The original spreadsheet window remains loaded in memory, but is hidden from view by the new window.

- /File|Open prompts you for a spreadsheet file name, then opens a new spreadsheet window and reads the specified file from disk into the new window. The new window is displayed with the position and size it had when last saved to disk.

New windows are assigned numbers, starting at 1, in the order they are opened. Each window also has a name: either the name of the spreadsheet file in the window, or the default SHEETn name assigned by Quattro Pro.

Window numbers

Selecting the Active Window

Only one window can be active at any one time. The active window is the only one that is affected by menu commands. There are three ways to change the active window:

- Select /Window|Pick or press the shortcut key, Alt-0. Quattro Pro displays a list of all open windows. Click the name of the desired window, or highlight it and press Enter. If the window is displayed, simply click it.

- To activate a window numbered 1–9, simply press Alt-n, where n is the number of the desired window.

- To make the next window active, press Shift-F6. This command steps through the windows in numerical order. The name of the active window is displayed in the lower left corner of the screen.

Zooming and Arranging Windows

If you have more than one window open, you have several options for displaying them on the screen.

Changing Window Size

You can modify the size of a window to allow more than one window to show on the screen at once. Figure 14.1 shows a Quattro Pro screen with three windows displayed.

To change window size with the keyboard:

1. Select /Window|Move/Size or press Ctrl-R, the shortcut key. The Move indicator will appear in the upper left corner of the active window. Press ScrollLock or . (period) and the indicator will change to Size.

2. Use the ↑ and ← keys to reduce the size of the window. Use the → and ↓ keys to increase size.

3. When the desired size is reached, press Enter.

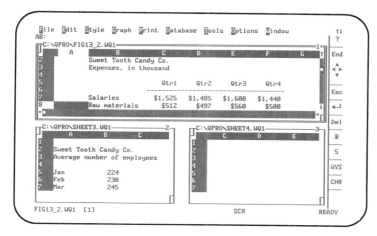

Figure 14.1: Multiple spreadsheets displayed simultaneously

To change window size with the mouse, point at the resize box in the lower right corner of the window, just below the vertical scroll bar's ↓. Press and hold the left mouse button, drag the window outline to the desired size, and release the button.

When a window is less than full size, it is enclosed in a double-line border. The file name associated with the window is displayed at the top left of the border, the window number is displayed at the top right.

Moving Windows

Windows that are less than full size can be moved, allowing you to position multiple windows for viewing.

To move the active window with the keyboard:

1. Select /Window|Move/Size, or press the shortcut key Ctrl-R. The Move indicator is displayed at the top left of the active window.

2. Use the arrow keys to move the window to the desired position and press Enter.

To move the active window with the mouse, point to any location on the window's double-line border. Press and hold the left mouse button, drag the window to the desired location, and release the button.

Stacking and Tiling Windows

Display-
ing all
open
windows
at once

When you have more than one window open, you may need to view all windows at one time. Quattro Pro offers two ways to do this: tiling and stacking. Tiling displays a small portion of each open spreadsheet in small, contiguous windows (Figure 14.2). Stacked windows are displayed in an overlapping stack, like you would hold a hand of playing cards (Figure 14.3).

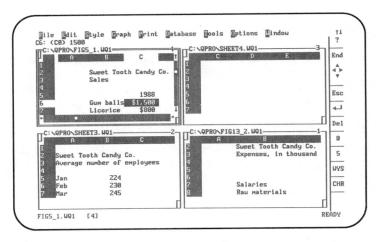

Figure 14.2: Tiled windows

To display all open windows:

1. For a tiled display, select /Window|Tile or press the short-cut key Ctrl-T.

2. For a stacked display, select /Window|Stack.

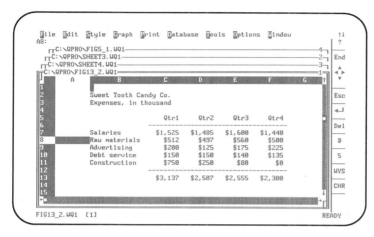

Figure 14.3: Stacked windows

When using a stacked or tiled window display, you select the active window as described earlier in this step. You can also resize and move windows.

Zooming the Active Window

The Zoom command lets you quickly zoom the active window to full-screen size. When the active window is less than full size, Zoom expands it to full-screen. When the active window is full-screen, Zoom returns it to its original size. To zoom, select /Window|Zoom or press the shortcut key Alt-F6.

Clearing or Closing a Window

When you are finished using the spreadsheet in a particular window, you can either clear or close the window. Clear erases all data from the window, making it available for you to start a new spreadsheet. Close removes the window from memory and from the screen display.

To clear or close a window:

1. Make the desired window active. Next, use either /File|
   Save or /File|Save As to save the spreadsheet
   to disk.

2. To clear the window, select /File|Erase. The window's
   spreadsheet is erased from memory, but the window
   remains displayed.

3. To close the window, select /File|Close. The window is
   removed from the screen.

4. To close all open windows, select /File|Close All.

When working with multiple spreadsheets, select /File|Save All to
save all open files. *Version 2 users:* This command is not available.

The Workspace

The locations and sizes of windows, and the files they contain,
constitute the *workspace*. You can save the Quattro Pro workspace
at any time. When you later retrieve it, the arrangement and contents of all windows will be restored exactly. This can be a great
time-saver when you frequently work with multiple spreadsheets.

To save the workspace:

1. Select /File|Workspace|Save. Quattro Pro prompts you for
   a name to be assigned to the current workspace. Enter a
   1–8 character file name; the file extension .WSP will be
   added automatically.

2. Press Enter and the current workspace will be saved to
   disk.

Saving the workspace does not automatically save the data in the
windows. You must use /File|Save to do this.

Using Spreadsheet Links

A *link* is a means by which a formula in one spreadsheet can reference data in another spreadsheet. For example, your Sales Projection spreadsheet may need some data from your Sales History spreadsheet. A link transfers the data automatically from one file to the other. When you create a link you specify both the name of the source file and the address of the source cell.

What is a link?

Linking to a Single Cell

A link to a single cell consists of the file name of the source spreadsheet in square brackets followed by the cell address. For example, if you enter

`+[SALES]A10`

in a cell, it will display the value in cell A10 in the spreadsheet SALES.WQ1. Similarly, the formula

`@SUM([SALES]A1..A10)`

will display the sum of cells A1..A10 in SALES.WQ1. When you enter the spreadsheet file name in a link formula, you do not need to specify the .WQ1 extension. If, however, the source is a Lotus 1-2-3 or Quattro 1 spreadsheet, you must specify the .WK1 or .WKQ extension as part of the file name. The file name can also include a drive and/or path specifier, if necessary.

Linking from Lotus 1-2-3 or Quattro 1 spreadsheets

Linking to a Block

You can link an entire block of cells to a block in another spreadsheet. This is easy because cell addresses in link formulas are relative and will adjust if you copy the formula to other cells. For example, you could enter the link formula +[SALES]A1 in cell B10 of the current spreadsheet, then use the /Edit|Copy command to copy that formula to cells B11..B20. The result would be:

B11 linked to [SALES]A2

B12 linked to [SALES]A3

...

B20 linked to [SALES]A11

The cumulative result is that block B10..B20 in the current spreadsheet is linked to block A1..A11 in SALES.WQ1. You can make a link formula cell address absolute by including dollar signs in the cell address, as discussed for regular formulas in Step 5.

Linking to a Named Block

If the source spreadsheet contains named blocks you can use the block names instead of cell addresses in the link formula. If the named block contains only a single cell you can use the name anywhere a single cell could be referenced; if the block contains multiple cells you can use it where multiple cells could be referenced. For example, say that the source spreadsheet SALES.WQ1 contains a single cell block named TOTAL and a multicell block named REGIONS. Table 15.1 shows examples of valid and invalid link formulas.

Link Formula	*Comments*
+[SALES]TOTAL	valid (single-cell source → single-cell destination)
@SUM([SALES]REGIONS)	valid (multicell source → multiple destination @ function)
+[SALES]REGIONS	invalid (multicell source → single-cell destination)

Table 15.1: Valid and invalid link formulas

Linking in the Workspace

If the source worksheet for a link formula is loaded into the workspace, you can simply point to the desired cell and Quattro Pro will automatically insert the file name and cell address in the formula.

To create a link to an open spreadsheet:

1. Move the cell selector to the cell that is to contain the link formula. Begin entering the formula, up to the point where the link reference is needed.

2. Press Shift-F6 until the source spreadsheet window is active. Move the cell pointer to the desired cell in the source spreadsheet. The source file name and cell address are entered in the formula.

3. Continue entering the formula or, if the formula is complete, press Enter. The original (i.e., destination) spreadsheet window becomes active again.

Step 16

Creating Databases

30

Quattro Pro can be used to maintain information in a *database*. A database is a storage method in which each item of information, or entry, has the same structure. Many common tasks, such as maintaining a mailing list, keeping track of sales records, or balancing a checkbook, are best performed with a database. This step uses an imaginary charity's list of its contributors and the amounts given as an example of a database.

What is a database?

Database Terminology and Structure

Database structure includes three major components:

- Each entry in a database is called a *record*. In a mailing list, each person's entry is one record. A Quattro Pro database holds one record per row.

- Every record is composed of one or more discrete *fields*. In our sample database, one field is devoted to each of the following: last name, first name, address, city, state, and amount contributed. Every record in a database contains the same fields. A Quattro Pro database holds one field per column.

- Every field is identified by a unique *field name*. A Quattro Pro database has its field names at the top of each column above the corresponding field.

Database components

Our sample database is shown in Figure 16.1. Most databases contain many more records than this, of course (Quattro Pro's limit is 8191 records).

When working with a large database, use /Window|Options| Locked Titles to keep the field names visible on the screen.

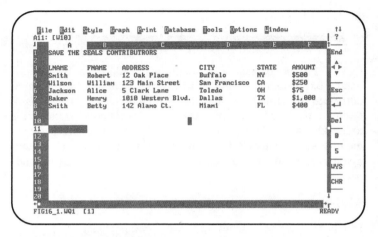

Figure 16.1: A sample database

Starting a Database

It's best to start with a blank spreadsheet when setting up a new database. While it's possible to keep more than one database in a single worksheet, I don't advise it. With Quattro Pro's multiple spreadsheet viewing ability, you will never need to anyway.

The first step in starting a database is deciding on the fields that each record will contain. Each separate item of data should have its own field. For example, instead of having a single Name field, last name and first name should be in separate fields.

Next, decide on field names. These must be unique for each field and should be descriptive of each field's contents. Make the field names as short as possible consistent with their being understandable.

Enter the field names starting in column A, one per column. You can put them in row 1 or, to leave room for an optional database title (as in Figure 16.1), in row 3.

Now you're ready to start entering data. The first record goes in the row directly below the field names. Do *not* leave a blank or decorative row between the field names and the first record; if you do so you will be unable to search for or sort information properly. Database data entry is the same as entering any other spreadsheet data.

Restricting Field Entries

You can instruct Quattro Pro to allow only certain types of entries in selected database fields. This can help to reduce errors and speed data entry procedures.

To restrict database entries:

1. Select /Database|Data Entry. A menu is displayed offering three options.

2. Select Dates Only to restrict entries to valid dates. Select Labels Only to restrict entries to labels. Select General to remove a restriction from a field restricted earlier to Dates Only or Labels Only.

3. Specify the block to be restricted. This will typically be the entire column containing the database field.

If you enter anything other than a valid date into a Dates Only cell, Quattro Pro beeps and enters EDIT mode. If you enter a date or a number into a Labels Only cell, it is converted to a label.

Step 17

Working with Databases

The usefulness of a Quattro Pro database is greatly enhanced by its ability to organize and manipulate the records in various ways. The two most frequently needed database tasks are sorting records in a particular order and searching for specific information.

Sorting a Database

Sorting a database means ordering its records based on the data in one or more fields. You could sort our sample database by last name to print an alphabetical list of contributors, or by amount given to find your most generous donors.

A Quattro Pro database can be sorted on one or more *sort fields*. A sort field is simply a database field whose data is used to order the records in the database. You can use as many as five sort fields. Records are first ordered according to data in the primary sort field. If there is identical data in the primary sort field (e.g., there is more than one Smith in your mailing list) the data in the secondary sort field is used. The sort process actually rearranges records in the spreadsheet so that the first record is in the first row, and so on.

Sort fields

To sort a database:

1. Select /Database|Sort|Block, then specify the block containing the records to be sorted. This block must contain all of the database records and fields, but must *not* contain the field names at the top of the columns.

2. Select 1st Key from the Sort menu. You can specify any single cell in the column containing the primary sort field or enter its field name. Next, select either Ascending or Descending order. If you need to use additional sort fields, specify them in the same way.

3. Select Go. The records are sorted and you are returned to READY mode.

Figure 17.1 shows the database in Figure 16.1, sorted with LNAME as the primary sort field and FNAME as the secondary sort field.

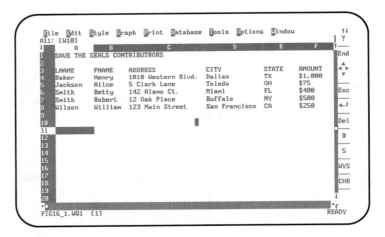

Figure 17.1: Sample database sorted by last and first names

If a sort operation gives unwanted results, you can use Undo (Alt-F5) to reverse it.

Quattro Pro's default is to sort in the following order (when Descending is selected this order is reversed):

1. Blank cells

2. Labels beginning with numbers in numerical order (based on the first digit only)

3. Labels beginning with letters or other characters in ASCII order

4. Values in numerical order

Formulas are sorted according to their calculated value, and dates are sorted as serial numbers. Select /Database|Sort|Sort Rules to change the sort rules. You have the following choices:

- Select Numbers Before Labels|Yes to place values before labels.

- Select Label Order|Dictionary to sort labels as they would be in a dictionary, disregarding case.

The default ASCII sort order will place all labels beginning with uppercase letters before those beginning with lowercase letters: Zoo before ape, for example. To get a true alphabetical sort, select /Database|Sort|Sort Rules|Label Order|Dictionary.

Select /Options|Update to save the new sort rules for future work sessions.

/Data|Sort can be used to order any spreadsheet data, such as a column of numbers.

Searching for Information

To search for specific information in a database, use the /Data-base|Query command. The Query menu is shown in Figure 17.2.

The process of searching, or querying, a database has three main steps:

1. Specifying the block of records to search.

2. Setting up search criteria to specify the information to be found.

3. Selecting the query operation to perform. Some operations require you to specify an output block first.

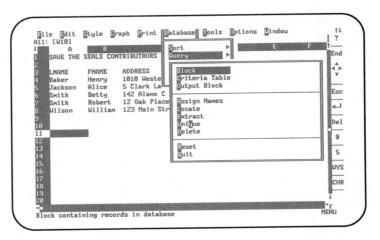

Figure 17.2: The /Database|Query menu

Specifying the Records to Query

To specify the block of records to be searched, select Block from the Query menu. Specify the spreadsheet block containing your database, including all fields and records and also including the row containing the field names. You can search a database in another open spreadsheet using standard linking syntax (e.g., **[SALES]A3..E100**).

*The Assign
Names
command*

Next, you can use the Assign Names command to assign block names to the cells in the first records. This step is optional, but highly advised because it greatly simplifies the procedure for setting up the search criteria. When you select Assign Names, the first data cell in each column is assigned that column's field name as a block name. For example, in the database in Figure 17.1, the Assign Names command would assign the name LNAME to cell A4, FNAME to cell B4, and so on.

To use the Assign Names command, field names must each be a single word and no longer than 15 characters.

Setting Up Search Criteria

Search criteria are what you use to tell Quattro Pro what information you are looking for. "Find all records where last name is Smith", or "Find all records where state is CA or NY" are two examples. Search criteria are entered in a *criteria table*. The criteria table is entered in a blank region of your spreadsheet and has two components:

- The top row of the criteria table contains database field names. This row can contain all the field names, but must contain at least the names of the field or fields you will be searching.

- Below the row of field names, the criteria table contains one or more rows of criteria. Each criterion is placed below the name of the field being searched.

This will be clearer if we look at an example. The spreadsheet in Figure 17.3 contains four criteria tables:

- The table in cells A11..A12 would find all records where the STATE field is CA.

- The table in cells A15..B16 would find all records where LNAME is Baker and FNAME is Henry.

- The table in D11..D12 would find all records where AMOUNT is greater than 500. In Figure 17.3, cell D12 has been formatted as Text so that the formula entered in the cell is displayed. Otherwise, the result of the formula as applied to the first database record would be displayed. In this case, 0 would be displayed because the first database record does not have AMOUNT greater than 500.

- The table in cells D15..D17 would find all records where CITY is Buffalo or Dallas.

Criteria table examples

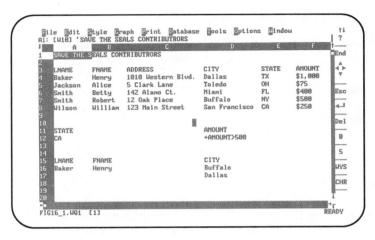

Figure 17.3: A spreadsheet with four criteria tables

While a spreadsheet can contain multiple criteria tables, only one will be used for any query operation. From the above examples, several rules about criteria tables can be seen:

- Place multiple criteria on the same row of the table if they all must be satisfied for a record to match (the LNAME, FNAME above).

- Place multiple criteria on separate rows of the table if any one (or more) of them being satisfied will result in a match (the CITY example).

- Use the relational operators < (less than), > (greater than), <> (not equal), ≥ (greater than or equal to), and ≤ (less than or equal to) to search for numerical values in certain ranges. The relational operators can also be used with labels to search for specified alphabetical ranges. For example, the criterion +LNAME< "B" will match all records with an LNAME entry beginning with "A". When used in relational criteria, labels must be enclosed in double quotes.

Once you have set up your criteria table, select Criteria Table from the Query menu, and specify the block containing the criteria table.

Specifying the Query Operation

Quattro Pro can perform several types of queries, which differ in what is done with the matching records. Two of these operations require only that you specify an input block and a criteria table, as explained above. Then, from the Query menu:

- Select Delete to erase all database records that match the criteria in the criteria table. Quattro Pro asks for confirmation, then deletes the matching records. Records below are moved up to fill the empty rows.

- Select Locate to find matching records. Quattro Pro highlights the first matching record in the database. You can use the ← and → keys to move between fields in the record, and use EDIT mode (F2) to make changes in the record. Pressing ↓ or ↑ moves the highlight to the next or previous matching record. To terminate Locate and return to the Query menu, press Escape.

The other two Query operations require you to specify an *output block* to which matching records will be copied. The output block can be any blank region of the spreadsheet containing a sufficient number of rows and columns to hold the copied records. The top row of the output block must contain the database field names. It can contain all of the field names or only a subset of them. In the latter case, only the corresponding fields will be copied by the Query operation.

Output blocks

To specify an output block, select Output Block from the Query menu, then specify the block. If you specify only the first row of the block (the one containing the field names), Quattro Pro will use as many rows below as needed (any existing data will be overwritten). Next (assuming you have already specified an input block and a criteria table), select the desired operation:

- Extract copies matching records from the database to the output block. Only those fields listed in the first row of the output block are copied.

- Unique works as Extract does but eliminates duplicate records from the output block.

Figure 17.4 shows our sample database after a /Database|Query|Extract operation. The criteria table is in A11..A12, and the output block is A15..F17. The two records where LNAME is Smith have been copied to the output block.

Note that an Extract operation does not change the original database in any way.

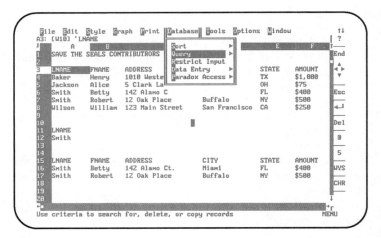

Figure 17.4: The results of a /Database|Query|Extract operation

Writing Macros

A *macro* is a series of recorded commands that can be played back to perform spreadsheet tasks. Macros can be extremely useful at all levels of complexity. At the simplest level, a macro could be used to save a few keystrokes every time you perform a common task. A more complex macro might be written to quickly format a spreadsheet in a certain manner. Quattro Pro's macro facility is powerful enough to write an entire application, such as an account ledger. What you can accomplish with macros is limited only by your imagination.

Macros save keystrokes and time

Recording a Macro

The most common type of macro consists of a series of recorded keystrokes. When you execute the macro, Quattro Pro responds just as if you had entered those keystrokes from the keyboard. For example, you may frequently need to format a column of numbers as Currency with two decimal places. If the cell selector is at the top of the column, the keystrokes required for this are:

```
/ S N C 2 {Enter} {End} ↓ {Enter}
```

That's nine keystrokes. If you recorded them as a macro, you could execute the same commands at any time with a couple of keystrokes.

To save a keystroke macro, use Quattro Pro's Record facility. When Record is on, any and all keystrokes and mouse actions you make are recorded. You can then paste the macro into the spreadsheet for later use. A spreadsheet can contain an unlimited number of macros.

Before trying out a macro operation, save your spreadsheet. If you make a serious mistake, you can retrieve the spreadsheet and start over.

To record a keystroke macro:

1. Plan the action you want to perform. You may wish to keep notes, or try a test run (after saving your spreadsheet of course).

2. When you are ready, select /Tools|Macro or press the shortcut key Alt-F2. The Macro menu is displayed. Select Record.

3. The REC indicator appears at the bottom right of the screen. Any keyboard or mouse actions you take are being recorded.

4. When you are finished, select /Tools|Macro or press Alt-F2, then select Record to turn recording off.

5. Check your spreadsheet to verify that the sequence of keystrokes you entered did in fact perform the desired action. If it did, you are ready to save your macro for future use.

Pasting a Macro

Saving a macro for later use

Once you have recorded a macro, the next step is to save it in the spreadsheet for future use. This process is called *pasting*. When you paste a macro, it is stored as labels in one or more spreadsheet cells, with special codes representing various commands and keystrokes. For example, the column formatting keystrokes given above would be pasted in three cells as follows:

```
{/ Block;Format}c2~
{END}
{DOWN}~
```

Many keystrokes are recorded as *menu equivalents* rather than as the actual keystrokes. For example, to change number format the first keystrokes are /SN. In a macro, this command is recorded as {/ **Block;Format**}. Similarly, the Enter key is recorded as ~, the ↓ key as{**DOWN**},and so on. Using equivalents rather than actual keystrokes makes recorded macros much easier to read and modify.

To paste a recorded macro:

1. Decide on a spreadsheet location for the macro. You should select a blank region that will not be disturbed by later data operations. Macros require a block one column wide; the number of rows depends on the macro's length. You can store the macro in another open spreadsheet if desired.

2. Select Paste from the Macro menu. Quattro Pro prompts you to enter a name for the macro. Enter a descriptive name using the standard rules for block names. This name can later be used to replay the macro. For macros you will be using frequently, assign a two-character name consisting of a backslash (\) followed by a single letter A–Z. Macros with a backslash-letter name are called *instant macros*.

3. Specify the block where the macro is to be stored. You can specify a single cell, and Quattro Pro will use as many cells below as are needed. If you are pasting to another open spreadsheet, use standard linking syntax to specify the block.

4. The macro code is pasted to the specified block, and the block name you entered is assigned to the first macro cell.

Replaying a Macro

You can replay, or execute, the most recently recorded macro using the Instant Replay command. This is done by selecting /Tools|Macro|Instant Replay or by pressing Alt-F2 followed by I.

To execute an instant macro, simply press Alt plus the letter key assigned to the macro. For example, to execute the macro named \D, press Alt-D.

To execute a noninstant macro, select /Tools|Macro|Execute or press Alt-F2| E. You then have three options:

1. Press F3 and select the desired macro name from the displayed list.

2. Use the arrow keys or mouse to point to the first cell in the macro block and press Enter.

3. Type in the macro's name or block address.

While a macro is in progress, you can stop execution and return to READY mode by pressing Ctrl-Break.

Editing and Debugging Macros

If a simple macro is not operating properly, you may be able to correct it by editing. A macro can be edited like any other spreadsheet label. Simply move the cell selector to the cell where the macro (or part of it) is stored and press F2 to enter EDIT mode. After you have fixed the mistake, press Enter.

A more complex macro may not be easily fixed by editing. You can use Quattro Pro's macro debugger. For details on the macro debugger, see the Quattro Pro documentation.

Autoexecute Macros

Creating an autoexecute macro

You may wish to have a particular macro execute every time you load the spreadsheet. This is done by assigning the macro name \0 (that's a zero, not an oh) to the macro. Each time the spreadsheet is loaded with /File Retrieve or /File|Open, the macro will be automatically executed.

You can change the autoexecute macro name with the /Options| Startup|Startup macro command.

Step 19

The File Manager

Quattro Pro's File Manager is a utility that manages files on your hard and floppy disks. The File Manager does not relate directly to spreadsheets or spreadsheet data, but it can be useful in managing spreadsheet files and other kinds of disk files. This step will teach you the most commonly used File Manager functions.

The File Manager Window

The File Manager functions in its own window. To open the File Manager, select /File|Utilities|File Manager. Like other Quattro Pro windows, the File Manager window can be resized, moved, and closed. To toggle between full- and partial-screen display, press Alt-F6. A full-screen File Manager window is shown in Figure 19.1; this window has the tree (explained below) open.

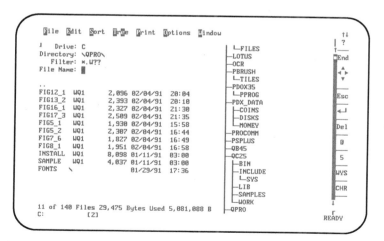

Figure 19.1: The File Manager window displayed full-screen

When the File Manager window is active, its menu is displayed on the top line of the screen. The File Manager window itself consists of three panes. The *control pane* is at the top of the window, and contains prompts for specifying disk drive, directory, file name filter, and file name. The *file list pane* displays a list of the files and subdirectories in the current directory. The *tree pane,* displayed by selecting /Tree|Open from the menu, displays a tree-structure diagram of the subdirectories on the current drive.

Activating a pane

To work in a pane, you must select it. The active pane displays an active cursor. To activate a pane, click it with the mouse or press F6 or Tab one or more times.

To close a File Manager window, make the window active and select /File|Close.

The Control Pane

The control pane contains four prompts that control the File Manager. These prompts have the following functions:

- Drive indicates the letter of the disk drive that File Manager is working with.

- Directory lists the directory whose contents are displayed in the file list pane.

- Filter is used to restrict files listed in the file list pane. The DOS wildcards * and ? can be used. For example, *.* lists all files, *.W?? lists all spreadsheet files (plus any other files whose extension starts with W), and *.WQ1 lists only Quattro Pro spreadsheet files.

- The Filename prompt is initially blank. If you enter the name of a spreadsheet file and press Enter, that file is opened and placed in a spreadsheet window. If you enter any file name (including wildcards) and press F5 (GOTO), the File Manager searches the disk for the specified file and, if it is found, displays the contents of the corresponding subdirectory.

To make a change to one of the control pane entries, activate the control pane, press ↑ or ↓ to move the highlight to the correct prompt, and press Esc to erase the current entry or Backspace to erase it one character at a time.

The Tree Pane

The tree pane displays a "tree" showing the subdirectory structure of the current disk. When you first activate the tree pane the current Quattro Pro directory is highlighted. If this is any directory other than the root directory, the path to it is highlighted as well. You can move the cursor to another subdirectory by clicking its name with the mouse. You can also use the cursor keys; use ← and → to move between levels, and use ↑ and ↓ to move within a level. The directory highlighted in the tree pane is the current File Manager directory. Its name is listed in the control pane, and its contents (based on the filter, if any) are listed in the file list pane.

The File List Pane

The file list pane lists the contents of the directory specified in the control pane and the tree pane. The list includes subdirectories (indicated by \) as well as the files that pass through the control pane filter. If you're in any directory other than the root directory, the file listing includes .. (this refers to the directory one level up). Each file listing shows the file name, its size in bytes, and the date and time it was created or last modified. You can change the order in which files are listed (by date or by size, for example) by selecting /Sort from the menu.

When you make the file pane active, the cursor will highlight a single file name (the cursor position is also indicated by a checkmark next to the file name). You move the cursor with the ↑ and ↓ keys. If the cursor is on the name of a spreadsheet file, press Enter to open the file. If the cursor is on the name of a subdirectory,

Selecting files

press Enter to move to that subdirectory. Other actions affect either the single file the cursor is on, or a group of two or more files you select as follows:

- Move the cursor to each additional file name and press Shift-F7 or + to select it (if it's already selected, this will deselect it).
- Click the file name with the mouse.
- Press Alt-F7 to select all files.

Once you have selected one or more files, you can delete them by selecting /Edit|Erase or pressing Del (be careful—deleting a file cannot be undone). To move the files to another directory on the same disk, select /Edit|Move or press Shift-F8. To copy the files to another disk and/or directory, select /Edit|Copy or press Shift-F9.

Moving and copying files

If you select Move or Copy, Quattro Pro displays the selected file names in a different color. You must next specify the destination for the Move or Copy operation. For a destination on the same disk, activate the tree pane, highlight the desired destination directory, and select /Edit|Paste or press Shift-F10. For a destination on a different disk (possible only with Copy), follow these steps:

1. Select /File|Utilities|File Manager to open a second File Manager window.

2. Make the control pane of the new window active and enter the destination drive letter after the Drive prompt.

3. Make the tree pane active and specify the destination directory.

4. Select /Edit|Paste, and the files selected in the first File Manager window are copied to the destination drive/directory.

Quattro Pro Options

15

Many aspects of Quattro Pro's operation are controlled by its options settings. Some options are set during installation, and a few others have been covered earlier in this book. This step explains the Quattro Pro options you are most likely to need to change.

Changing Printers

If you change your system printer after installing Quattro Pro, you need to inform Quattro Pro about the change so that reports and graphs will print properly. Remember that Quattro Pro can have one or two printers installed at the same time.

To change the Quattro Pro printer setting:

1. Select /Options|Hardware|Printers, then select either 1st Printer or 2nd Printer, depending on which printer you are changing. A menu is displayed listing the make, model, and mode of the currently installed printer. From this menu select Type of Printer.

2. Select your printer's manufacturer from the displayed list. Another list is displayed, from which you select the printer model.

3. For most printer selections, a list of printer modes is displayed. This offers options for paper size, print density, and so on. Select the desired printer mode from this list.

4. Press Esc three times to return to the Options menu, then select Update to save the new printer settings. Finally, select Quit to return to READY mode.

Color Options

If you have a color video system you can customize the colors that Quattro Pro uses for various screen elements. To modify colors select /Options|Colors. Next, select the Quattro Pro component to modify: Menu, Desktop, Spreadsheet, Help, or File Manager. A list of elements is displayed. For example, in Spreadsheet you can control the color of cells, labels, borders, and so on. Select the element to modify and a color chart appears from which you select foreground and background color.

Conditional colors

Select Conditional from the /Options|Colors menu to set the colors used to display particular spreadsheet values. You could, for example, display negative values in red and positive values in blue. To display conditional colors you must select /Options/Colors| Conditional|On/Off|Enable. Conditional colors are displayed only if the color palette is selected.

Startup Options

Select /Options|Startup to control Quattro Pro's startup procedure. This menu command lets you specify the name of the autoexecute macro, the name of a spreadsheet file to load automatically, the menu structure to use (your choices are Lotus 1-2-3, Quattro 1, or Quattro Pro), and the default data directory, among other things.

Format Options

Select /Options|Formats to specify the default spreadsheet formats. The choices available are:

- Numeric Format specifies the default numeric format to be applied to value cells.

- Align Labels specifies the default label alignment.

- Hide Zeros determines whether values of zero are displayed or not.

- Global Width specifies the default column width.

Updating Your Options

After you make changes in options settings, they will remain in effect for the remainder of the current work session. To keep them in effect for future work sessions as well, select Update from the Options menu.

If you want to see a list of the status settings that are saved by the /Options|Update command, select Values from the /Options menu. The list displayed also shows the current values of the options. *Version 2 users:* The /Options|Values command is not available.

Index